the diabetes
WEIGHT LOSS DIET

the diabetes
WEIGHT LOSS DIET

antony worrall thompson
azmina govindji • jane suthering

photography by steve baxter

Kyle Books

This book is dedicated to the two million people with diabetes and to those who could also be at risk.

IMPORTANT NOTE

The information and advice contained in this book are intended as a general guide to dieting and healthy eating and are not specific to individuals or their particular circumstances. This book is not intended to replace treatment by a qualified practitioner. Neither the authors nor the publishers can be held responsible for claims arising from the inappropriate use of any dietary regime. Do not attempt self-diagnosis or self-treatment for serious or long-term conditions without consulting a medical professional or qualified practitioner. It is vital that you talk to your diabetes care team about losing weight before you start and have regular reviews of your progress.

This edition published in 2008 by Kyle Books
An imprint of Kyle Cathie Limited www.kylecathie.com
Distributed by National Book Network, 4501 Forbes Blvd., Suite 200, Lanham, MD 20706 Phone: (301) 459 3366
Fax: (301) 429 5746

Recipes © 2007 Antony Worrall Thompson, except for pp44 left, 47 left, 48 right, 49 left, 50 left, 53, 54 right, 58 top left and right, 61, 62, 65, 67, 68, 70, 73, 124 left, 130-141 © 2007 Jane Suthering
Text © 2007 Azmina Govindji
Photography © 2007 Steve Baxter
Book design © 2007 Kyle Cathie Limited

First published in Great Britain in 2007 by Kyle Cathie Limited
www.kylecathie.com

ISBN 978-1-904920-76-2
10 9 8 7 6 5 4 3 2 1

Antony Worrall Thompson, Azmina Govindji and Jane Suthering are hereby identified as the authors of this work in accordance with Section 77 of the Copyright, Designs and Patents Act 1988.

EDITORIAL DIRECTOR Muna Reyal
DESIGNER Jenny Semple
PHOTOGRAPHER Steve Baxter
HOME ECONOMIST Jane Suthering assisted by Anna Helm
STYLING Rachel Jukes
COPYEDITOR Marion Moisy
RECIPE ANALYSIS Dr Wendy Doyle
PRODUCTION Sha Huxtable and Alice Holloway

Library of Congress Control Number: 2008923098.

Color reproduction by Sang Choy
Printed and bound by CraftPrint

contents

THE RECIPES

A word from Antony

There's dieting and there's your diet, two words with very different meanings. Dieting means losing weight whereas diet is the food you eat on a day-to-day basis. What I've tried to do with this book is combine the two so that you can eat well and lose weight at the same time.

A few years ago, I was told that I was at an increased risk of diabetes. Of course I worried that my food life was over so I did some research and realized people with diabetes can still eat well as long as they follow some basic rules. I initially wrote **Healthy Eating for Diabetes** followed by my **GI Diet** (Glycemic Index) and **GL Diet** (Glycemic Load), which were aimed at people who wanted to eat healthily, especially those with diabetes. Many of us are keen to lose weight and this book, while following the good food principles of my previous books, will also help you to achieve this.

I've managed to lose about 28 pounds and I want to lose another 15, but I'm not into instant "bikini" diets – they are not sustainable in the long term, are no good for your health, and you usually put back on all the weight you lose. I've also been really pleased with the results of my last three books. So many readers have told me that they have lost weight and some have even managed to reduce or come off their diabetes medication. These are results we should all be proud of and I'm sure this book will have a similar effect.

This diabetes weight loss diet isn't a quick fix. It's a diet that is healthy and will improve your well-being as well as your weight and equally importantly I reckon you're going to enjoy it, which will be a bonus. Follow the menu plans, mix and match recipes if you want, but always remember to keep an eye on the calories. The food is so enjoyable you may be tempted to ask for second helpings, so be disciplined, learn to enjoy smaller portions – your body will soon get used to it. Temptation is one of life's biggest enemies so when you go shopping for food, write lists and wear blinders!

My final message to you is to eat well, lose weight, stay healthy, and enjoy yourself.

ACKNOWLEDGEMENTS

There are too many people to thank but certain individuals deserve a special mention: My wonderful wife, Jacinta and our two children, Toby and Billie, who suffered from my lack of quality time yet supported me throughout, as well as moving house and office during this period! To Louise Townsend, my energetic and ultra-efficient PA, who fielded hundreds of phone calls from the publishers and who was regularly on hand to smooth troubled waters when the pressures of deadlines took their toll. To my agents, Fiona Lindsay and Linda Shanks at Limelight Management, who keep me from being idle. To my teams at Notting Grill, Barnes Grill, Kew Grill, The Lamb, and The Greyhound, and in particular, David Wilby, my Operations Director, who kept the boat(s) afloat. To Azmina Govindji, who yet again has done excellent nutritional work, and to Jane Suthering. To Jenny Semple, the designer, and Steve Baxter, the photographer, who have made this book look so good. And finally to Muna Reyal, my editor, an iron hand in a velvet glove, and her great team at Kyle Cathie.

Antony Worrall Thompson

So many people are involved when a new book gets published – it isn't just about the authors. I would like to express my gratitude to my dear friend and colleague Dr Wendy Doyle who has tirelessly helped with the recipe analysis and menu plans. I was assisted with research for this book by Rajni Jambu, student dietitian working with Aparna Srivastava RD, Senior Lecturer in Dietetics at Coventry University. Thank you also to Sue Baic RD from Bristol University, Jacqui Troughton, Advanced Diabetes Practitioner, and the Nutrition and Dietetic Services of Leicester Royal Infirmary. Mountains of appreciation go to my co-authors – we make a cracking team! And huge thanks to our colleagues at Diabetes UK, especially Natasha Marsland, Jemma Edwards and Zoë Harrison from the Healthcare and Policy Team, and to Muna Reyal of Kyle Cathie Publishers, for being so patient and for your guidance throughout this project.

Azmina Govindji BSc RD

Team work is everything on a project such as this. In the kitchen I have been ably assisted by Anna Helm. Wendy Doyle and I have spent many hours balancing the recipes to fit the necessary dietary criteria and the editorial help from all at Kyle Cathie is unsurpassed. I thank you all.

Janie Suthering

This section will explain how diet can affect your diabetes and how losing weight can help you to manage it as well as bring you other health benefits.

about the
diabetes
weight loss diet

Introduction

Congratulations for picking up this book! You have taken the very first step in making a difference to your health and your day-to-day life. Being overweight can seriously affect your health, but there are also many other reasons to lose weight. Making realistic long-term changes to your lifestyle can bring huge rewards – whether you want to fit into last year's summer clothes, play in the park with your children, or run for the bus, losing weight (and keeping it off) is worth the effort. As you flick through these pages, you will find tempting recipes and practical tips to help you do this – but remember that you should check with your healthcare professional before going on a diet.

This book is intended for people with diabetes who need to lose weight. However, it is also a great resource for anyone who wishes to eat more healthily or reduce the risk of Type 2 diabetes. By trying out these tasty recipes, which have all been created specifically with health, blood glucose control, blood pressure, and heart health in mind, you will be better equipped to reduce your risks of developing Type 2 diabetes, especially if you're overweight. Since eating for diabetes is simply a healthy diet, the whole family can enjoy this delicious dining experience. Take a look at the tips in the following pages to help support you with your new healthy lifestyle goals.

If you have Type 1 diabetes, your condition will be managed with insulin as well as a healthy diet and physical activity. At least 30 percent of people with Type 2 diabetes are on insulin, too. Since the recipes and menus (see pages 38–41) are intended for people who want to lose weight, if you are not overweight you will need to allow yourself larger portions. There are also recipes that are intended for weight maintenance, indicated at the top of each recipe by a green marker.

DIABETES – WHY TREAT IT?

Over twenty million people in the US have diabetes. However, 6.2 million (nearly one-third) are completely unaware of it. Often diabetes can be picked up when you go to the doctor for a routine checkup and it is important to speak to your doctor if you have any of the symptoms listed below.

CLASSIC SYMPTOMS OF DIABETES

- Passing urine more regularly, especially at night

- Increased thirst

- Extreme tiredness

- Genital itching or regular episodes of thrush

- Slow healing of wounds

- Recurring infections such as boils

- Blurred vision

- Weight loss, usually in people with Type 1 diabetes

People with Type 1 diabetes produce no insulin and therefore require insulin injections as well as a healthy diet and regular physical activity in order to manage their diabetes.

Type 2 diabetes develops when your body can still make some insulin but not enough, or when the insulin that is produced doesn't work efficiently enough. It usually occurs in people over 40 years old, though in people of South Asian and African-Caribbean origin, it often appears after the age of 25. However, recently more children are being diagnosed with the condition. Type 2 diabetes is treated with a healthy diet and increased physical activity. Tablets and/or insulin may also be needed.

RISK FACTORS FOR TYPE 2 DIABETES INCLUDE

- A family history of diabetes
- Being overweight and inactive or with a waist measurement over a certain size (see page 16)
- Ethnic origin – South Asian and African-Caribbean people are more at risk
- Gestational diabetes (diabetes during pregnancy)

To find out more, visit the American Diabetes Association website; www.diabetes.org

THE INSULIN CONNECTION

When you eat food, some of that food is broken down into glucose (sugar) during digestion. The glucose then flows into the bloodstream where it is circulated around the body and subsequently used up by your muscles. As soon as glucose enters the blood, a signal goes to your pancreas gland to allow your body to release the hormone insulin. Insulin helps glucose to move from your blood into your muscles or liver where you can use it for energy or store it for later use.

Blood glucose is normally very carefully controlled by insulin. But in Type 1 diabetes, no insulin is produced and in Type 2 diabetes, not enough is produced or the insulin produced is not working properly (this is called insulin resistance) and often your blood glucose level will rise above the normal range. The aim of eating well and having a healthy, active lifestyle is to help to keep blood glucose within a healthy range. The American Diabetes Association currently recommends that people with diabetes aim to keep their blood glucose levels at 70-130 mg/dl (5.0-7.2 mmol/l) before meals and at no higher than 180 mg/dl (10.0 mmol/l) two hours after meals.

The good news is that you can help to manage your blood glucose levels in Type 2 diabetes by making small, simple changes to your lifestyle. In both types of diabetes, the main aim is to achieve healthy blood glucose levels as well as blood pressure and cholesterol that is as near normal as possible. This, together with a healthy lifestyle, will improve well-being and protect against long-term damage to the eyes, kidneys, nerves, and major arteries. Being overweight makes diabetes control more difficult as excess weight makes it hard for the body to use insulin properly. Losing weight will help diabetes control for both Type 1 and Type 2.

Since people with diabetes are more prone to heart problems, it is especially important to reduce the risk of heart disease by stopping smoking if you smoke, and monitoring blood pressure and blood fat levels. A healthy lifestyle and losing weight can significantly reduce your cardiovascular risk.

The plan

No doubt you've tried many other diets – and no doubt the weight has just crept back on again. This is a classic pattern for people who get sucked into quick-fix diets. But the good news is that by making sustainable changes to your lifestyle today, you can live a full life. The key here is the word "sustainable." And no change in your behavior is going to last if it means making drastic changes to your day-to-day habits. And that is why this plan is right for you:

▓ You love your food! You're tempted by the enticing photographs and you enjoy and savor your meals. With this plan, you can have your cake and eat it. Every recipe has been created with good health and a balanced diet in mind, and the menus have been designed to help you lose weight slowly and steadily while indulging in your favorite foods. A weight loss plan can only succeed in the long term if you enjoy it.

▓ Every recipe has been carefully analyzed and the ingredients used are in accordance with healthy eating recommendations. Simply keep to the portion sizes and cooking methods suggested; this will help to ensure that you are having a healthy balance of foods that are low in saturated fat and that contain slowly digested carbohydrates that help to keep your blood glucose levels steady throughout the day.

▓ We suggest regular meals and healthy snacks, so you really don't feel you're on any sort of diet! This isn't about restriction, it's about enjoyment. And when you're eating regularly, you're more likely to be performing at your best and to have good energy levels throughout the day. Now that must be good for your self-esteem, too!

▓ This plan includes healthy low glycemic index (GI) foods such as beans (legumes), lentils, whole grains, nuts, seeds, pasta, and plenty of fruits and vegetables. Since these foods can take longer to digest, they can help you feel fuller for longer while keeping your blood glucose levels steady.

▓ This is not a quick-fix diet and the menu plans do not cut out any food groups. It's simply a way to kick-start a healthy balanced lifestyle, appropriate for the whole family.

▓ All in all, the simplicity and attractiveness of this plan means that you're more likely to keep to it.

Weight-watching, why bother?

Around 80 percent of people who have Type 2 diabetes are overweight, and it's likely that they carry this excess weight around their waist. This extra weight causes the body's insulin to be less effective, creating a greater risk of developing diabetes. So if you already have diabetes and are overweight, then losing weight, especially from the tummy area, will improve your body's sensitivity to insulin, which will make it work more effectively. And if insulin works better, your blood glucose is likely to be under better control. Good news all around!

BENEFITS OF WEIGHT LOSS

- Improves blood glucose levels

- Lowers blood pressure

- Lowers unhealthy blood fats (triglycerides, LDL – low-density lipoprotein or "bad" cholesterol)

- Reduces risk of long-term complications of diabetes

- Improves mobility

- Gives you a sense of well-being and improves your self-esteem

THE LOWDOWN ON BLOOD GLUCOSE

Diabetes is a condition where blood glucose is abnormally high, so it doesn't take a genius to work out that any steps that help to keep blood glucose levels within a healthy range will improve the overall control of diabetes. When you eat carbohydrate foods such as bread, potatoes, rice, and sugary foods, they are digested into glucose which then passes into the bloodstream. If you have diabetes, the insulin in your body is less able to transport the glucose from the blood into your muscles where it can be used for energy. So if you have untreated diabetes, your blood glucose remains high.

Losing weight, even small amounts of weight, together with a healthy diet and physical activity, will help to improve how sensitive you are to insulin (see "The 10 Percent Factor," page 18). And by watching what and when you eat, you will be able to influence the rise and fall in your blood glucose levels. This, in turn, will improve your "glycemic control," which simply means that it will help to minimize fluctuations in your blood glucose levels. This way, you will be less likely to suffer the symptoms of highs and lows in your blood glucose and this can improve your long-term health.

Your diabetes medication should match the food you eat and your level of activity. As you lose weight and become more active, you become less resistant to insulin your body produces or that you inject, therefore whether you have Type 1 or Type 2 diabetes you may need to have your diabetes medication dose reduced. Some people with Type 2 diabetes who lose weight as a result of their lifestyle changes are able to control their diabetes with less or without any diabetes medication. Diabetes is a lifelong condition and their diabetes hasn't been cured, but it has been controlled through food and physical activity. As Type 2 diabetes is a progressive condition, medication may be needed in the future to control your blood glucose levels.

HOW CAN I TELL IF I NEED TO LOSE WEIGHT?

In this book, we give you simple, practical steps on how to lose weight gradually and keep it off, but for now let's establish how much weight you need to lose in order to make a significant improvement to your health.

Calculate your BMI

(Reproduced with kind permission from Jacqui Troughton, Advanced Diabetes Practitioner, Leicester Royal Infirmary, UHL (www.leicestershirediabetes.org.uk)

Your body weight as well as your shape is likely to affect your health. The Body Mass Index (BMI) is used internationally by health professionals to assess whether your weight could be putting your health at risk. You can work this out by multiplying your weight in pounds by 703, and dividing that number by your height in inches. Then divide the result again by your height in inches. This means that if you weigh 150 pounds and are 5'5" tall, your BMI will be [150 ÷ (65)^2] x 703 = 24.96.

HEALTH RISK ASSOCIATED WITH BODY MASS INDEX (BMI)

	BMI	BMI (Asian origin)	Health Risk
Underweight	Less than 18.5	Less than 18.5	
Normal	18.5-24.9	18.5-22.9	
Overweight	25-29.9	23-24.9	Increased
Obese	30.0-34.9	25.0-29.9	High
	35.0-39.9	30.0-34.9	Very High
Morbidly obese	Greater than 40	Greater than 35	Extremely High

If you fall into the overweight, obese or morbidly obese categories, your weight is putting your long-term health at risk, so by reading this book, you are taking your first steps to doing something about it.

HOW DO YOU SHAPE UP?

Although your weight is a very useful indicator of long-term health, more and more research is pointing to the importance of where your fat is distributed and how that can have significant effects on health. Carrying too much weight around the middle, or central obesity (also sometimes referred to as apple-shaped), can increase the risks of developing heart disease and high blood pressure. There is extensive research to show that people who are centrally obese tend to be less sensitive to the effect of insulin. This can then lead to a condition called insulin resistance and people who have insulin resistance tend to be more prone to developing diabetes. People with diabetes are likely to already be less sensitive to insulin and so if your excess weight is carried around your middle, it is particularly important to take steps now. As you can see from the waist circumference guidelines below, you do not need to be very apple-shaped to be at increased risk.

If you carry your weight on your hips rather than on your waist, you are likely to be pear-shaped, and this is a less detrimental way to carry excess fat. But the most important measurement is your waist and you should work towards meeting the guidelines below. You can do this by eating a range of healthy foods within a calorie-controlled diet and by engaging in regular physical activity.

MEASURING YOUR WAIST CIRCUMFERENCE

By measuring your waist you can get a good idea if you have excess fat around your waist. Stand with your feet hip distance apart and take the measurement between the top of the hip bone and the lowest rib. The tape needs to be snug but it shouldn't compress the skin and needs to be parallel to the floor. Breathe out before the waist measurement is taken.

WHAT SIZE DO YOU TAKE?

A study published in the *Journal of Human Nutrition and Dietetics* in 2005 looked at clothing size and whether this might be a parameter in assessing health risks. Some 200 men and 160 women took part in a research project in Glasgow, Scotland. Detailed measurements such as waist circumference, BMI, and blood pressure were taken.

The BMI score is the standard marker for describing obesity in populations, but in clinical practice, waist circumference measurement is a more accurate method of predicting risk. High-waist circumference and BMI values as indicated below and on page 15 were found to be strongly linked to clothing size. What's especially fascinating (and useful) is that the cut-off points for increased health risk related to US waist size were 34 pants for men and a US dress size of 12 for women (size 14 in the UK). "High risk" cut-offs were size 36 pants for men and a dress size of 14 for women (size 16 in the UK).

The bigger the sizes in your closet, the greater the risk of heart disease – in the research study, pants over waist size 38 in men indicated a nearly four-fold chance, and women with a dress size above 16 (size 18 in the UK) had a seven-fold chance of having at least one of the main cardiovascular risk factors.

YOUR GENDER & RACE	INCREASED HEALTH RISK AT THIS WAIST MEASUREMENT
White and African-Caribbean men	37 inches or above
Indian and Pakistani men	35 inches or above
All women	31 1/2 inches or above

The 10 percent factor

Your goal in managing your diabetes is to keep blood glucose levels steady throughout the day and in the long term. This helps to prevent the long-term complications of diabetes such as heart, eye, and kidney problems. Minimizing fluctuations in your blood glucose levels can also help your day-to-day health and improve the quality of your life as you begin to feel better both physically and mentally. Eating well throughout life makes good sense, and it's not about setting yourself unrealistic weight loss targets. The best news is that, if you are overweight, by losing just 5-10 percent of your weight, you can make a major contribution to improving the quality of your long-term health.

THE SCIENCE BIT

The dietary guidelines in this book are based on scientific evidence. We have interpreted the research for you and translated it into practical advice. There is extensive research to show that if you are overweight, losing weight leads to a significant improvement in your blood glucose levels and there are no two ways about it. What's interesting is that there is now research to show that losing just 10 percent (based on someone weighing 220 lbs losing 22 lbs) carries considerable health benefits.

There is good evidence to suggest that in people who need to lose weight, a moderate weight loss of 5-10 percent of body weight will have a major impact on the long-term complications of obesity. Weight reductions of 10-20 lbs in someone who weighs 220 lbs have been shown to improve back and joint pain, as well as symptoms of breathlessness.

A large study, called the UK Prospective Diabetes Study (UKPDS), carried out over a 20-year period on more than 5,000 people with Type 2 diabetes, was published in the *Lancet* in 1998. The results showed that, in people who weighed 220 lbs, weight loss of 22 lbs can achieve greater reductions in HbA1c (the longer-term predictor of how well your blood glucose is doing) and fasting blood glucose (after you have not eaten for at least 8 hours) than treatment with the diabetes medication metformin alone. For people with diabetes, the weight loss also reduced the need for blood pressure and lipid-lowering treatment (medication to lower blood cholesterol and triglyceride). These findings don't necessarily mean that you would not need treatment any more if you were to lose weight, but that you need to check with your healthcare team to see.

A comprehensive review of studies on weight reduction of 10 percent or less was published in the *International Journal of Obesity* in 1992. The studies indicated that in obese people with Type 2 diabetes, a 10 percent weight loss appeared to improve blood glucose control and reduce blood pressure and cholesterol levels. Modest weight reduction also appeared to increase length of life.

A recent UK study on overweight and obese adults published in the *British Medical Journal* suggested that a weight loss of 10 percent was possible and reasonable over 6-12 months and had beneficial effects on health.

Changing your diet, activity levels, and losing weight could help to reduce the dosage of your diabetes medication.

If you are overweight, even a 5 percent loss of body weight can improve insulin action, decrease fasting blood glucose concentrations, and reduce the need for diabetes medications. Data from the Diabetes Prevention Program (DPP) published in the *New England Journal of Medicine* in 2002 demonstrated that weight loss (of 7 percent in the first year) and increased physical activity (2¹/₂ hours of brisk walking per week) was nearly twice as effective as drug treatment with metformin in preventing diabetes in people who already had raised blood glucose levels.

Participants in the Diabetes and Obesity Intervention Trial (DO IT, conducted by the University of Pittsburgh) who achieved a 10 percent weight loss after six months were able to match the weight loss of another group of people who also took a weight loss drug (Orlistat). In fact, 18 out of 25 people who were taking diabetes medication at the start of the study were able to stop taking their medication! We obviously cannot guarantee that you can expect these results; remember that people in a research study are carefully monitored so that they keep to the dietary and physical activity changes recommended. However, anyone who is overweight can benefit from losing just 10 percent of their body weight. And that's a fact.

In short, if you lose 10 percent of your body weight, for instance by reducing your weight from 220 lbs to 198 lbs, you could enjoy the following health benefits:

- Improved blood glucose levels
- Lower blood cholesterol and triglycerides (types of blood fats)
- Reduced blood pressure
- Less back and joint pain
- Reduced risk of angina
- Less breathlessness
- Improved sleep
- Improved self-esteem and confidence

For many people with diabetes, changing their diet and activity levels and/or losing weight could help to reduce the dosage of diabetes medication required, so you will need to liaise with your healthcare team before and during your weight loss program.

If you are able to improve your insulin sensitivity (and this amount of weight loss should certainly help to do that), then you will have a better chance of keeping your blood glucose levels under control and hence this may help you to reduce the amount of diabetes medication you currently take. If you are not on any diabetes medication, then any weight loss will certainly help to reduce your need for it in the future.

Are you really ready?

No doubt you've tried diets in the past. If you've had a diagnosis of diabetes in the family, you may have been motivated to eat more healthily. If you simply wanted to lose weight for your looks, no doubt you've tried various diets which might have had short-term results. So what's different this time? This book is not about another diet – it's about healthy eating. But first things first: this section will enable you to explore how motivated you are today, and this will help you to gauge whether you are really ready to take on this healthy lifestyle. You will lose weight only if you make sustainable changes to your normal everyday habits – what you eat and how active you are.

GETTING STARTED: WEIGHT-LOSS MOTIVATION ASSESSMENT

Try the quiz below to see how motivated you are. It will help to assess how important weight loss is to you, at this particular stage in your life. Weight loss is important to me because:

FOR MY HEALTH

My doctor says I should ☐

I think it would improve my symptoms ☐

I don't want my health to get worse ☐

I need to lose weight before an operation ☐

Because activity makes me breathless ☐

Because I have difficulty with dressing/undressing ☐

Because I can't fit into seats in planes, buses ☐

Because I can't keep up with my partner/children ☐

To set an example for children/grandchildren ☐

To have more energy to enjoy life ☐

To feel better about myself ☐

To have more control over my life ☐

To make someone else happy ☐

Because I am embarrassed about being overweight ☐

FOR MY APPEARANCE AND SOCIAL LIFE

I think I will look better ☐

Others want me to look better ☐

I will be able to wear nicer clothes ☐

To be more attractive to my partner ☐

To improve job opportunities ☐

To feel able to enjoy a normal social life ☐

You may have other reasons, so use the space below to remind yourself:

_____

_____

_____

_____

_____

If your reasons for losing weight are mainly to do with other people, for example your doctor, partner, or friend, then this can be less helpful than if the reasons are important to you personally. If weight loss is more important to you than to others, then you are more likely to succeed – as you are if you have the support of other people.

Once you have identified your reasons for wanting to lose weight, it can be helpful to think about the following questions:

1 Why do I want to lose weight now?

2 What would be the good things about making changes in order to lose weight? (e.g., I will have more energy)

3 What would be the more challenging aspects about making changes in order to lose weight? (e.g., I don't enjoy exercise and will have to do more)

4 What would be the good things about staying as I am? (e.g., no effort is needed)

5 What would not be good about staying as I am? (e.g., the arthritis in my knees will get worse)

Spending time giving some thought to these questions could be very helpful because you will have a more realistic idea about your motivation and the things that might get in the way of success. If, for example, you have a long list of answers to questions 3 and 4, then it is possible that your motivation is low at the moment. However, if you have a long list of answers to questions 2 and 5, then your motivation is probably high.

Questions 3 and 4 will help you see any barriers to losing weight. If there are practical difficulties to overcome, you can work on solutions to these with your dietitian or nurse.

WILLPOWER BOOSTERS

■ If you think something is going to be difficult to achieve, it will be! This time, see your new healthy lifestyle plan as something to be embraced; something that you really want here, today, now, as you know it will have benefits for you and your family.

■ If you find that you have a bad day in terms of your food or activity choices, simply acknowledge the lapse and start again. You don't need to wait till Monday to get back on track!

■ Make a list of all the benefits you will achieve once you have lost weight successfully and kept it off. Keep this list handy to remind yourself.

■ Think about how your self-confidence may change once you have lost the weight.

■ Will you be any different at work when you achieve your goals?

■ How will being healthier affect your relationships and how you behave around people whom you care about?

If you feel after having done this quiz that you are not ready to take on a weight loss plan, then let it go, wait a while, and come back and review this when you feel more ready. Trying to lose weight if you are not really ready can often be counterproductive.

Guidelines for the weight loss diet

Our eating plan is based on national recommendations for healthy eating. However, it is no substitute for personalized dietary advice for diabetes. If you have been diagnosed with diabetes, it is imperative that you visit a registered dietitian for advice that is tailored to your needs. If you have not already seen a registered dietitian, ask your doctor to refer you to one. He or she will be able to assess your current eating habits and help you with specific advice to improve the control of your diabetes and also to lose weight. Always speak to your doctor before embarking on any weight loss plan.

1 EAT THREE REGULAR MEALS

Avoid skipping meals, and spread your breakfast, lunch, and evening meal over the day. This will not only help you control your appetite but also assist in controlling your blood glucose levels. Another associated benefit of this control is that it will help to improve your mood and concentration.

This plan encourages you to eat breakfast, lunch, and dinner, with light snacks in between. We have designed the plan so that you are in total control of what you eat and also so that you are able to enjoy really tasty home-cooked foods.

Remember that extra snacks can pile on the pounds so choose low-calorie ones like fruit or lowfat yogurt where possible. There is also a chapter of recipes for healthy homemade snacks.

For some people who take diabetes medication, snacks are essential – check with your dietitian or doctor if this applies to you. It is also important to talk to your healthcare specialist as it may be possible to adjust your diabetes medication so that you don't need to snack between meals.

The other important thing about eating regularly is that you won't be so inclined to reach for the cookie jar because you will find that you are less hungry. There is research to show that eating small, regular meals can help to keep your blood glucose levels stable and even help you to consume fewer calories.

2 EAT MORE FRUIT AND VEGETABLES

OK, so you've heard it all before. Despite the fact that US Dietary Guidelines promote the importance of eating at least five fruits and vegetables a day (5 A Day for Better Health), current intakes in the US are still averaging between two and three portions. All of us, whether we have diabetes or not, should aim for at least five portions a day, but many people are confused by exactly how much a portion is.

RISE AND FALL OF BLOOD GLUCOSE LEVELS

BLOOD GLUCOSE

breakfast · mid-morning snack · lunch

TIME OF DAY

Here are some examples of a portion:

- Medium-sized fruit, such as an apple, banana, or orange
- 1 large slice melon or pineapple
- 2 plums, apricots, tangerines, or kiwi fruit
- Handful of grapes or cherries
- 3 tablespoons fresh fruit salad or canned fruit in natural juice
- ½ a grapefruit or avocado
- 1 tablespoon dried fruit, such as raisins, apricots
- 1 glass (²/₃ cup) unsweetened fresh fruit juice (counts only once as one of your five a day)
- 3 tablespoons raw or cooked vegetables
- 1 dessert bowl of salad
- 3 heaping tablespoons beans and legumes (count only once as one of your five a day)

You will notice that a large majority of the recipes in this book have some fruit or vegetables as part of the ingredients list, which will help to count towards your five a day.

Remember also that fruit and vegetables are nature's power foods. They are rich in a wide range of vitamins and minerals and in fiber, and for the most part are also low in fat and calories. In short, as part of a weight loss plan, they are your best friends. In terms of disease prevention, there is extensive research to show that eating more fruit and vegetables can reduce your risks of developing heart disease, some types of cancer, and gut problems.

3 INCLUDE STARCHY CARBOHYDRATE FOODS WITH EACH MEAL

People with diabetes are advised to choose foods that help to keep their blood glucose levels steady. This includes eating carbohydrates or starchy foods (bread, pasta, chapatis, potatoes, yams, noodles, rice, and cereals) that are digested and absorbed as glucose into the bloodstream.

The amount of carbohydrates you eat is important in the control of your blood glucose levels. All varieties of carbs are fine but try to include those

THREE KEY POINTS ABOUT FRUIT AND VEG

- Eat a wide range of different colored fruits and vegetables. By ensuring you have a good variety, you are more likely to get a wide range of nutrients. For example, orange-colored apricots, papaya, and carrots will provide the antioxidant beta-carotene, while red tomatoes will provide cancer-protective lycopene.

- Potatoes don't count, because they are considered to be a starchy carbohydrate food and they don't have the range of nutrients you would normally find in fruit and vegetables. Beans and legumes (see above left) do count, but only as one portion.

- Fresh, frozen, canned, dried, and juiced fruits and vegetables all count, so look for different ways to include them in your diet – a glass of juice for breakfast, a spoonful of dried fruit over your cereal, and, of course, vegetables with every meal.

that are more slowly absorbed (i.e., have a lower glycemic index) as these won't affect your blood glucose levels as quickly. Diabetes advice has always focused on choosing low glycemic index (GI) carbohydrates, but since 2004 the GI has hit the headlines for its successful results for weight loss and its overall health benefits.

Essentially the GI is simply a measure of how quickly foods that contain carbohydrates raise your blood glucose levels. If you have diabetes, eating more foods containing slowly absorbed carbohydrates can help to even out blood glucose levels. There are extensive tables listing GI values of foods. However, it is not necessary for you to know individual GI values. What's important is that you choose those foods that will offer glycemic benefits, that is, slow, steady rises in your blood glucose level after meals.

Using GI on its own is not appropriate, as you also need to think about how many carbohydrates you're eating. Your blood glucose is determined by both the quality of the carb (GI) and its quantity. The glycemic load (GL) is calculated by taking the percentage of a food's carbohydrate content per portion and multiplying this by its GI value. It gives you a more accurate indication of how your blood glucose will be affected by a particular serving of food, so it is a reflection of both the quality and quantity. This is helpful when thinking about foods with a high GI, like watermelon. Although it has a high GI rating, a slice is actually quite low in carbohydrate. So the GL of a serving of watermelon is low and this is a perfectly acceptable food. Focusing on the GL on its own is not appropriate for diabetes, because it is possible to follow a low GL diet by simply eating less carbohydrates – and these carbs could be high GI. Research suggests that the link between low GL diets and good blood glucose levels is the consumption of low GI foods, not low carbohydrate intake. In short, you don't need to get bogged down by GI figures or GL; simply eat those carbs that offer you the best blood glucose response, and watch your portion sizes.

GI TIPS FOR DIABETES

■ Eat regularly. How nice does that sound?

■ Make sure you eat three meals a day. Breakfast is really important as it helps to steady your blood glucose after the overnight fast. If you ensure you choose a low GI breakfast, you're less likely to be tempted by unhealthy snacks later.

■ Choose at least one low GI carbohydrate (see opposite page) at every meal, and ideally at snack times, but remember to watch portion sizes to keep the GL low.

■ Get into the habit of piling vegetables onto your plate. For weight loss, half your plate should be filled with vegetables. In the other half, fill two thirds with starchy foods like rice, pasta, and potatoes, and fill the final third with protein foods like lean meat, fish, beans, lowfat cheese, or tofu.

■ Base your desserts on fruit. You will find a tempting array of fruity endings to your meals in this book.

■ A little careful planning goes a long way. Scan our list of healthy low GI foods and keep some handy. You'll find that our snack recipes are great for a quick pick-me-up.

■ The beneficial effects from a low GI meal can run into the following meal, which helps keep blood glucose more even during the whole day.

■ Make sure you eat more vegetables. And if they are only lightly cooked, they are likely to be more slowly digested, which will help with your glycemic control. You'll end up doing more chewing, which will make you feel more satisfied, and because your plate will look fuller, this will make you feel you're eating more.

All great psychological tips to enhance your motivation!

Lower GI Choices

BREADS

Choose seeded, multi-grain, rye, soy, and linseed. Whole-wheat bread and white bread are both considered to be high GI foods because the flour is more refined and this makes the bread more quickly digested and absorbed. The key is to choose foods that need more chewing, so a seeded bread with the whole-wheat grains intact will offer you a far better blood glucose result than whole-wheat or white bread. And eating it with lower GI foods (such as baked beans) will be even better.

OTHER STARCHY ACCOMPANIMENTS

Basmati rice, brown rice, and some varieties of long-grain rice (such as easy-cook) offer a medium GI rating. Sticky rices such as jasmine and risotto tend to make blood glucose rise more quickly. With any type of rice, try to cook it until just tender rather than mushy.

Most types of pasta do very well on the GI scale. Choose pasta regularly and cook till al dente because if it is overcooked, it will have a higher glycemic index. Remember though to keep to the amounts given in the recipes in this book, and to team it up with other low GI accompaniments like a side salad.

Potatoes tend to have a higher GI rating, especially if mashed or overcooked. Choose new potatoes boiled in their skins or try sweet potatoes. This doesn't mean that mashed potatoes are off the menu – simply team them up with a low GI food such as baked beans or coleslaw in a reduced-calorie dressing.

Experiment with different types of grains. Bulgur, quinoa, oats, and couscous are all excellent choices.

LEGUMES

Beans and lentils, such as kidney beans, lima beans, chickpeas, and red and green lentils are fantastic and count once a day as part of your five fruit and vegetables recommendation. Try adding them to stews, casseroles, and soups, or to a salad.

FRUITS AND VEGETABLES

Most fruits and vegetables offer a low GI rating, so enjoy them regularly. Whenever possible, have them raw and whole rather than cooked.

GO FOR LOW GI FOODS AS PART OF A BALANCED DIET

One of the reasons why GI has not been taken up extensively is that the research as it currently stands is based on the blood glucose response after eating a single food. So, for example, we know that the GI value of whole-wheat bread is high when it is eaten on its own. However, we don't normally do that. As soon as you put some ham and lettuce and tomatoes into a whole-wheat sandwich, you lower its consequent GI value and hence its effect on your blood glucose. Also, your glycemic load will be different depending upon whether you eat one or two slices – two slices will have a greater effect on your blood glucose levels.

If your diet doesn't include many low GI foods, you could end up with more highs and lows in your blood glucose levels, which is not desirable. This is why it's really important to include as many low GI carbohydrates in your diet as possible. And if you can, choose those low GI foods that are fresh and natural, like oatmeal, legumes and lentils, pasta, and so on, because you'll know that you're also getting a good range of nutrients.

❹ BE FAT-WISE

Weight for weight, pure fat has more than twice the calories of pure protein or carbohydrate. So, it makes sense to eat less fat if you want to lose weight. You may think lowfat food is boring, but there is a wide array of herbs, spices, lowfat marinades, and more that can add zest and taste to lowfat dishes – just check out the recipe for Indonesian jumbo shrimp curry (page 88) if you need reassurance.

Research from the Mediterranean countries shows that people who eat diets rich in mono-unsaturated fats such as olive oil, avocados, nuts, and seeds do seem to have lower risks of heart problems. Obviously, there is more to this than just the type of fat eaten, and other lifestyle and cultural factors will be at play. However, it is fine to enjoy small amounts of monounsaturated oil in cooking and that's what you'll be doing when you try out our mouth-watering dishes.

Choose lower-fat cooking methods such as baking, grilling and broiling, poaching, and roasting without fat. You may enjoy some lowfat manufactured foods, such as fat-free dressings, low-fat spreads, and so on. These are all fine as part of a healthy balanced diet; however, you will find that the recipes in this book will provide you with tasty dressings and treats that are also low in fat and without that processed taste. And a great trick is to make your own spray oil using olive or canola oil. Simply invest in a pump spray bottle (available from most good household stores) and pour your favorite oil into the bottle. This way you are likely to use less oil when spraying from a bottle than when pouring. Or use a brush dipped in oil to lightly coat your ingredients or pan.

TYPES OF FAT

Fats are an essential component of the diet, but too much of certain types can lead to a build-up of fatty streaks in the arteries, which can reduce blood flow to the heart. One of the main risk factors of coronary heart disease is high blood cholesterol. If you eat foods that cause your blood cholesterol to rise, you're more likely to suffer from heart problems.

There are two types of cholesterol in the blood:
■ **high density lipoprotein** (HDL) represents "good" cholesterol – the higher your HDL, the lower your risk of heart disease;
■ **low density lipoprotein** (LDL) is often called "bad" cholesterol – a high LDL level can increase your risks as it leads to the formation of fatty deposits in the arteries.

Certain types of fat will have an effect on your HDL and LDL levels. Remember that it's firstly important to cut down on the amount of fat you eat. Within this, aim in particular to reduce those foods that are rich in saturated fat, as this is linked to heart disease. Choose unsaturated fats or oils, especially monounsaturated fat found in olive oil and canola (rapeseed) oil, as these types of fat reduce LDL blood cholesterol. Saturated fat and trans fat do the opposite, so cut down on foods that contain these (see below).

■ Saturated fats. Usually found in fatty meat, full-fat dairy products, butter and lard, ghee, coconut oil, and palm oil.
■ Trans fats. These are found in some processed foods such as cakes, cookies, pies, and pastries. You may see them listed on an ingredients list as hydrogenated vegetable fats.
■ Monounsaturated fats. Found in olive oil and canola oil, and spreads based on these oils. Although these are healthier fats, it's still important to watch your overall fat intake.
■ Polyunsaturated fats. Include sunflower oil, corn oil, and soybean oil, and margarine and spreads based on these oils. These have been shown to lower blood cholesterol levels and therefore help in reducing the risk of heart disease, but, weight for weight, all fats and oils have the same number of calories, so it's still important to limit amounts. Oily fish contain polyunsaturated fats that are essential for your well-being as your body cannot make them.

5 GET YOUR OMEGAS
Oily fish is rich in a particular type of essential fat called omega 3. These fish oils have been shown to be protective against heart disease because they help to reduce blood stickiness and can also help to reduce a particular type of blood fat, called triglycerides. Aim to eat at least two portions of oily fish a week. Examples include salmon, trout, herring, tuna, mackerel, pilchards and sardines but canned tuna does not contain any of these good fats as they are destroyed in the canning process.

6 DON'T PASS THE SALT!
High blood pressure makes you more prone to heart conditions. Since eating too much salt is linked with high blood pressure, and people with diabetes are more at risk of high blood pressure, cutting down on salt makes a whole lot of sense.

Salt is the common name for sodium chloride and it is the sodium part of salt that is harmful if taken in excess. Adults should limit their sodium intake to 2,400mg or less a day; this is equal to a teaspoon of fine-grain salt or nearly two teaspoons coarse kosher salt. Most of the salt you eat comes from processed food, and it is very likely that you are taking in far more than this amount each day, especially if you rely heavily on processed meals and snacks.

■ Measure the amount of salt you add in cooking and if necessary, gradually cut down the amount you use. The recipes in this book allow you to taste the natural flavors as added salt is kept to a minimum.

■ Avoid adding salt at the table. Choose pepper, paprika, and other spices instead.

■ Experiment with herbs and spices, using for example freshly ground spices, dried and fresh herbs, paprika, and freshly ground black pepper, and you won't miss the taste of salt.

■ For varied flavors, try lemon and lime juice, balsamic vinegar, and Tabasco.

■ Choose products that have a reduced-salt content, for example tuna canned in spring water rather than brine, and unsalted butter and reduced-salt condiments.

■ Cut down on salty foods such as salted chips, nuts, savory crackers, and salty pastries. Choose fresh fruit, unsalted nuts, and unsalted popcorn as alternative snacks.

■ Salted and smoked foods such as bacon, sausages, smoked fish, some canned fish, and other processed convenience foods are often loaded with salt. Whenever possible, use fresh foods such as fish, lean meat, fruits, and fresh vegetables. They only have a small amount of salt present naturally.

■ Read food labels carefully. Salt may be listed as sodium, sodium chloride, mono-sodium glutamate, or bicarbonate of soda (baking soda).

7 LIMIT THE SWEET STUFF

Eating well doesn't mean saying goodbye to sugar. Sugar can be used in foods and in baking as part of a healthy diet. However, choose sodas that are sugar-free (such as fruit-flavored seltzers), have no added sugar, or are labeled "diet" since sugary drinks cause blood glucose levels to rise quickly.

8 ALCOHOL

It is recommended that women drink no more than two units of alcohol a day and men no more than three units. If you are watching your weight, remember that alcohol contains empty calories so it is best to limit your alcohol intake to about one unit a day and to include a few alcohol-free days a week. One unit of alcohol is equivalent to a 10-ounce glass of normal-strength beer, or a shot of liquor (about 1 fluid ounce). You might find that a 10-ounce glass of certain beers now contain about $1\frac{1}{2}$ units of alcohol, and a 6-ounce glass of wine, as much as two units.

Try alternating your alcoholic drink with a seltzer or low-calorie soda, or making your drink go further by adding club soda or having a mixed drink of 1 shot of liquor and the rest of a diet soda. Also, try to have eight glasses of fluid each day, including water, tea, coffee, sugar-free drinks, and squashes.

Never drink alcohol on an empty stomach, as it can cause hypoglycemia (low blood glucose levels) if you are taking certain diabetes medication. And remember never to drink and drive.

9 DIABETIC PRODUCTS – WHO NEEDS THEM?

Steer clear of any foods labeled specifically for people with diabetes. They tend to be expensive and often contain just as much fat or calories as standard versions of the same food. What's more, the types of sweetener used in these products may have a laxative effect and can still affect your blood glucose levels.

Shop till you drop...
...a waist size that is!

Shopping for food is good; the more you shop for food, hopefully the less you will rely on take-out meals. It's what goes into your shopping cart that might need a closer look. No doubt the recipes in this book will entice you into buying choice ingredients that will help you to savor your food and enjoy a range of healthy meals. This section will give you further guidance on how to make speedy yet sensible supermarket choices.

Reading a label may not be the most attractive pastime when you're rushing around trying to buy tonight's dinner. So here are some very quick tips to help you be a little bit more discerning as you scan the shelves.

1 A LITTLE OR A LOT?

Nutritional information given on food packaging can be used to tell whether a food has a little or a lot of fat, salt, fiber, or sugar. The table below gives you the guidelines for interpreting whether the amount represents a lot or a little for each 100g. However, when you look at the nutritional label, you will often see the information displayed as per serving, with grams given in parentheses after it. Therefore, make sure you check the serving size and how many servings you are actually consuming. (Also see the sample label on page 31.)

HOW TO TELL IF A PRODUCT CONTAINS A LITTLE OR A LOT OF A PARTICULAR NUTRIENT

This is a lot (per 100g)	This is a little (per 100g)
10g of sugars or more	2g of sugars or less
20g of fat or more	3g of fat or less
5g of saturated fat or more	1g of saturated fat or less
3g of fibre or more	0.5g of fibre or less
0.5g of sodium or more	0.1g of sodium or less
1.25g of salt or more	0.25g of salt or less

2 FOOD LABELS – NUTRITION FACTS

In the US, all processed foods must carry food labels displaying specific nutritional information to help the consumer determine the make up of that food. The nutritional information on American food labels is based on an average serving while in the UK, nutritional information is based on a 100g amount. When following the information on the American labels, you should check to see whether the amount of your average serving is the same as the amount given on the label – the "average" serving of ice cream is often only about one scoop so don't assume that what is an average serving for you will be the same size as that listed on the label.

American food labels list on the left-hand side the gram amounts for the categories appropriate to that food, for example: total fat (and of that, saturated fat), cholesterol, sodium, total carbohydrate (and of that, dietary fiber and also sugars), protein. On the right-hand side they list the "% Daily Values." The Daily Values are based on a 2,000-calorie diet so you can easily see what percent of these values the categories of this food comprises. In other words, if it says the total fat of a single serving is 25% of the Daily Value, then one serving contains a quarter of your daily recommended allotment of fat. The "% Daily Value" column makes it easier to compare one product with a similar one, so that if you're watching say, your fat or sodium intake, you can choose the product that has less.

The Daily Values shown at the bottom of the label list the minimum daily amounts one should consume (as with fiber) and the maximum (as with saturated fat). Although the "% Daily Values" column is based on a 2,000-calorie diet, The Daily Values at the bottom of the label give the recommended amounts for both a 2,000-calorie diet and a 2,500-calorie diet, so you can guage what's appropriate for you and your level of activity.

Sample label for Macaroni and Cheese

NUTRITION FACTS
Serving Size 1 cup (228g)
Servings Per Container 2

Amount Per Serving

Calories 250	Calories from Fat 110

	% Daily Value*
Total Fat 12g	18%
Saturated Fat 3g	15%
Trans Fat 3g	
Cholesterol 30mg	10%
Sodium 470mg	20%
Total Carbohydrate 31g	10%
Dietary Fiber 0g	0%
Sugars 5g	
Protein 5g	
Vitamin A	4%
Vitamin C	2%
Calcium	20%
Iron	4%

*Percent Daily Values are based on a 2,000 calorie diet.
Your Daily Values may be higher or lower depending on your
calorie needs

*THE DAILY VALUES

Calories
250

This is the amount of calories in one serving

10%

This is the percentage of your daily calorie allowance that one serving will provide

	Calories:	2,000	2,500
Total Fat	Less than	65g	85g
Sat Fat	Less than	20g	25g
Cholesterol	Less than	300mg	300mg
Sodium	Less than	2,400mg	2,400mg
Total Carbohydrate		300g	375g
Dietary Fiber		25g	30g

3 FANCY A TOUR?

Some supermarkets run shopping tours led by a registered dietitian. They last about an hour and visit different sections of the store, looking at healthy choices for people wanting to manage diabetes and lose weight. You can learn how to understand the information given on food labels and how to compare products to make healthy choices. Ask the store manager or your local community dietitians if diabetes store tours are available in your area.

If you do not have access to these store tours, remember that your shopping cart should ideally be filled with more whole foods than processed foods. Check out the Lower GI Choices section (page 25) for some quick tips on what to buy, and see overleaf for some more ideas.

■ Choose reduced-sugar/low-sugar foods and sugar-free drinks when shopping. When buying foods containing sweeteners, choose those with intense (also commonly known as artificial) sweeteners, e.g., saccharin (954), aspartame (951), acesulfame potassium (950), and sucralose (955). If you do use sweeteners, choose a variety.

■ Avoid "diabetic" products that contain nutritive sweeteners (sorbitol, maltitol, mannitol, isomalt, xylitol) as these have no more benefit to people with diabetes than ordinary ones. Diabetic products can be just as high in fat and calories as ordinary versions and therefore can still affect your blood glucose level. Furthermore, these sweeteners can have a laxative effect if eaten in excess.

■ On food labels, the list of ingredients is always given in descending order of amount. The higher up an ingredient is on the list, the more of that ingredient is contained in the food.

■ Be aware that there may be several types of fat, sugar, or salt in the ingredients list − hydrogenated vegetable oil, corn oil, cocoa butter, and milk fat are all types of fat; sucrose, invert sugar syrup, and molasses are all types of sugar. Salt content may be listed as salt or sodium chloride, and salt is present in MSG (monosodium glutamate) and stock.

■ If possible, take a detour so you don't need to pass the chocolate/confectionery aisle and the snacks sections. And it's best not to shop when you're hungry as the sight and smell of bakery goods might be a little too challenging to resist!

■ You may be less tempted by unhealthy choices if you make a shopping list and stick to it.

FAT-O-METER

Amount of saturated fat found in different types of cheese – based on a serving

Highest in saturated fat

Cream cheese

Parmesan

Brie

Edam

Cheddar cheese *reduced fat*

Mozzarella *reduced fat*

Ricotta

Feta *reduced fat*

Cottage cheese, plain

Quark

Lowest in saturated fat

SALT-O-METER

Amount of salt found in different types of snacks – based on a serving (portion weight given in brackets)

Snacks highest in salt

Tortilla chips (50g)

Bombay mix (30g)

Cornflakes (35g)

Reduced-salt potato chips (30g)

1 low-salt crispbread (10g)

Plain unsalted popcorn (75g)

1 unsalted cracker (7g)

Unsalted nuts (25g)

Fruit and vegetable crudités (80g)

Snacks lowest in salt

SUGAR-O-METER

Amount of sugar (total) found in different types of snacks – based on one serving

Highest in sugar

Sweetened soft drinks

Ice cream

Fat-free frozen yogurt

Candy

Jelly donut

Cakes with cream filling

Chocolate chip cookie

Oatmeal cookie

Crackers

Lowest in sugar

TIPS FOR HEALTHY EATING OUT

◼ Avoid bar nibbles such as peanuts, chips, and so on.

◼ When ordering food, ask for any sauce or dressing to be left off or served on the side.

◼ Order extra portions or large portions of vegetables/salads – and of course bread rolls (ideally grainy bread) if your meal doesn't have enough carbohydrates for your needs – or if your meal is delayed.

◼ Ask if portions of salad/vegetables can be substituted for less healthy options.

◼ Avoid ordering fried foods, dishes in pastry shells, and dishes with creamy sauces. Go for tomato-based sauces instead.

◼ Order skinless chicken or ask for the skin to be taken off. If it comes to your table with the skin on, just remove it neatly and set aside. You will reduce the calories in your meal by doing this.

◼ Stop eating once you are full, even if it means leaving some food on your plate. Ask the waiter to remove your plate as soon as you have finished so you are less likely to pick at any leftover food.

◼ If you have wine with a meal, dilute it with sparkling water or alternate it with diet soft drinks.

◼ Choose a fruit-based dessert.

Move more!

You don't need to go to the gym or jog every day in order to start becoming more active. Just incorporate the "move more" strategy into your everyday life. Moving more simply means standing up to change the channel on your TV rather than reaching for the remote, it means going upstairs to get one thing immediately rather than waiting till you need three or four things, it means getting up from your desk to refill your water or coffee. Every little action you take will have a cumulative effect on your daily energy expenditure and the more you increase your expenditure, the more effective your weight loss is likely to be. But before you start any new activity, talk to your doctor – especially if you are taking any medication for diabetes or heart disease; have any complications of diabetes such as foot or eye problems; are not sure which activities suit you; or have any conditions that may restrict your mobility or ability to be active.

IT'S A SIMPLE EQUATION:

If the food you eat (energy taken in) is less than the amount you expend (energy used up), you will **lose weight.** Your aim is to achieve a calorie or energy deficit.

Physical activity isn't just about weight loss. Take a look at this list of additional benefits of increasing your activity levels:

- Improves your diabetes control and helps to prevent some of the complications of diabetes
- Improves muscular strength and increases flexibility
- Prevents and manages high blood pressure
- Reduces lower back pain and strengthens the back
- Helps to reduce anxiety, tension, and stress
- Increases self-esteem and confidence
- Supports maintaining a balanced and healthy diet
- Helps to beat the blues
- Helps to keep up a healthy body image and good sex life
- Improves your cholesterol levels
- Helps with weight management
- Reduces the risk of heart disease, osteoporosis, and cancer

Physical activity is often linked with a healthy self-image and it can, with a little practice, become second nature. The key is to choose an activity you enjoy and that fits in with your day-to-day life! If much of your day is spent behind a desk, or in a stuffy environment, you just might feel lethargic and tired. Believe it or not, injecting some physical activity into your day can actually make you feel fresher and more energized. So moving around, ideally in the fresh air, can have a beneficial impact on your mood. Think about doing some activity as soon as you finish work or at home, as soon as you get in. Even ten minutes makes a difference.

The recommended **minimum** amount of activity for adults is 30 minutes on at least five days of the week. If you're normally inactive and are now keen to build up your stamina and fitness levels, it's best to seek advice from your doctor. Otherwise, gradually build more movement into your daily routine. Here are some ideas:

- First have a goal. It's only when you have a target that you will be really motivated. You could choose to have a daily or weekly aim, but make it realistic and specific and write down how you will make it happen. For example, "I will go for a brisk walk for 20 minutes three times a week."

■ Think of household chores and gardening as your ways to increase your energy expediture and aim to make them more vigorous (for instance, moving furniture to vacuum underneath, or mow the lawn, or dig the garden).

■ Carry shopping bags to your car rather than using a shopping cart. Or park the car further away from the supermarket.

■ Walk or cycle to work.

■ Try activities with the family, such as swimming, bowling, cycling, a walk, or a game of baseball or football in the park.

■ Do simple exercises while watching TV or listening to music (gentle jogging on the spot, stretches, lunges, abdominal exercises, pelvic floor exercises, contracting your buttocks, etc.).

■ Make an appointment with yourself to exercise on a weekly/daily basis and make sure you keep your appointment! To help keep yourself motivated, keep a record of your progress, gradually build on this, and make a note of how it makes you feel afterwards. Treat yourself (with something other than food) if you are keeping to your goal. Set ongoing rewards for your achievements – a new CD, a glossy magazine, a new book, or a trip to the movies when you've achieved a step towards your goal.

Exercise log

WEEK:

Goal/aim for this week:
e.g., walk to work three times a week, use the stairs instead of the elevator

DATE	TYPE OF ACTIVITY e.g., walking	EXERCISE TIME e.g., 20 minutes	DISTANCE e.g., 1 mile	ANY COMMENTS
Total time of exercise				

About the recipes

These recipes have all been specially created and nutritionally balanced so at first you will want to follow them exactly – and so you should! However, don't be afraid to alter them slightly by substituting one herb for another. There's also a wealth of different grains, legumes, and pastas, so do experiment.

Hopefully, all the ingredients in these recipes are available in your local supermarkets. Having said that, they all do have different ranges of products so you may have to shop around to some extent. An occasional trip to a health food store is also well worthwhile. In some cases we have been quite specific about an ingredient. We recommend:
- whole-wheat flour with malted grain
- multi-grain bread

IN YOUR PANTRY, KEEP A STOCK OF...

- cans of beans in WATER – without added salt or sugar
- cans of chopped tomatoes
- jars or cans of roasted red peppers – always drain and rinse well before use
- dried pasta – try alternatives such as wholewheat, spelt, and kamut
- brown rice – particularly brown basmati
- noodles – rice, rice and quinoa, buckwheat (soba)
- grains – couscous, quinoa, barley, wheat berries or spelt wheat berries, and bulgur
- rolled oats
- seeds – linseed, hemp, pumpkin, sunflower, or sesame
- dried fruits – raisins, apricots, or prunes
- nuts – almonds, pine nuts, and hazelnuts, but choose the natural varieties which are unsalted

IN YOUR FREEZER, KEEP...

- peas
- soybeans
- fava or lima beans
- spinach
- corn

- cage-free, organic eggs
- lowfat milk
- yogurt – no-fat Greek yogurt or plain
- olive or canola (rapeseed) oil
- citrus fruits

READ THE LABEL – IT'S QUITE AN EYE OPENER!
- Don't assume that all "light" cheeses have the same number of calories.
- Check the salt content of "lowfat" or "extra-lean" products – often salt is added as a balance to the loss of flavor from the lack of natural fats in the meat.

TRICKS OF THE TRADE
- Invest in a fine (microplane) grater – Parmesan goes a long way when it's finely grated.
- Slice meats thinly.
- Use a smaller plate (eat slowly and chew well).

COOKING
- Use nonstick pans wherever possible and a light spray of oil as necessary.
- Add a splash of water to stop ingredients sticking.
- Grill or broil, steam, or bake wherever possible.

BUTTER
This appears very occasionally in this book. It's a natural product and we prefer to use it in our recipes to give the best results and flavor. You may prefer to use a polyunsaturated or a monounsaturated spread to replace the butter. If so, use it in equivalent quantities to the specified amount of butter; however do be aware that it may give a slightly different result.

BREADS
Note that salt levels are usually much higher in commercially prepared breads, so as often as possible, do try to make your own (see pp49 & 66).

About the menu plans

**Welcome to your tailored and tasty menu plans.
Our Weight Loss Plan has been designed to help
you lose weight slowly and steadily, at the rate
of about 1 to 2 pounds per week. This is followed
by a sensible Weight Maintenance Plan, which
will help you to maintain a healthy weight.**

Each day has been carefully designed to help
ensure a balanced amount of carbohydrates
and other nutrients, while keeping your fat, salt,
and sugar intake within acceptable limits. There
is no need for you to worry about doing any
calculations; these have all been done for you.

YOUR MENU GUIDELINES

1 Plan ahead so that you have the ingredients
ready for making your meals each week.

2 The menu plans run for seven days, but this
doesn't mean that you need to eat exactly the
same food every week; it is simply an example of
how you can achieve an appropriate calorie intake.

3 The weight maintenance recipes have been
given a special logo as they are slightly higher in
calories and more appropriate for the time when
you have achieved your target weight.

4 If you are losing more than 2 pounds a week on
the Weight Loss Plan, or still losing weight on the
Weight Maintenance Plan, then it is better for you
to eat a little more to slow down your weight loss.
Think about having extra fruit, lowfat yogurt, lowfat
milk, or carbohydrates such as seeded bread,
basmati rice, or pasta to supplement the menu plan.

5 You need three servings of calcium-rich foods
daily. This has been taken into consideration when
devising the menu plans, although if you prefer to
swap the snacks or desserts for lowfat yogurt or a
skinny latte, then this will help you to achieve your
daily targets. Any milk listed separately in the
menu plans is in addition to the milk allowance.

6 You can bulk out your meals with extra
vegetables except legumes, corn, peas, and root
vegetables. Also allowed are tea, coffee, other

drinks made with milk (from the allowance), and
artificial sweetener; diet soft drinks, low-cal drink
mixes, and sugar-free sparkling water and mixers.

7 Alcoholic drinks have been included in the
menu plans. It's important to keep to the limits as
described on page 28, but the calorie contribution
from alcohol has been included in both plans. This
will allow you to have four units of alcohol a week
during the Weight Loss phase and ten units a week
during the Weight Maintenance phase.

Although calorie needs for men and women do
vary, these plans are based on 1,500 calories per
day for the Weight Loss phase and 2,000 calories
per day for the Weight Maintenance phase. If you
are a moderately active man or active woman,
you may wish to allow extra snacks or larger
portions during both phases. This is not intended
as a weight-reducing diet for children; however
the recipes are healthy, delicious, and appropriate
for children. You may wish to give active children
larger portions and extra healthy snacks.

Weight loss plan

MONDAY	TUESDAY	WEDNESDAY
Breakfast Quick banana sandwich (p. 49)	**Breakfast** Banana and cinnamon oatmeal (p. 44) with fruit	**Breakfast** Tropical fruit tabbouleh (p. 44)
Mid-morning snack Dill and buttermilk roll (p. 66)	**Mid-morning snack** Apricot mug loaf, 1 slice (p. 68)	**Mid-morning snack** Chili bean pâté (p. 67) with celery stalks
Lunch Bean and salad wrap (p. 94) **Dessert** Mango fool (p. 140)	**Lunch** Smoked trout kedgeree (p. 83) **Dessert** 7 ounces berries and $^2/_3$ cup lowfat yogurt	**Lunch** Curried veg and lentil soup (p. 76) **Dessert** Afghan cardamom puddings (p. 133)
Mid-afternoon Oat thin (p. 58) and milky drink ($^2/_3$ cup lowfat milk)	**Mid-afternoon** Spiced seed mix (p. 61) and $^3/_4$ cup fat-free fromage frais	**Mid-afternoon** 4 graham cracker cookies (p. 61)
Dinner Asian calf's liver (p. 126) **Dessert** Anna's iced berry crush (p. 133)	**Dinner** Steak with beans and greens (p. 106) **Dessert** Souffléed pumpkin pie custard (p. 130)	**Dinner** Spiced cod (p. 105) **Dessert** Roasted peaches with blueberries (p. 138)
Bedtime Hot chocolate nightcap (p. 73)	**Milk for the Day** 1$^1/_3$ cups skim or 1 cup lowfat	**Bedtime** Hot chocolate nightcap (p. 73)
Milk for the Day 1 $^1/_3$ cups skim or 1 cup lowfat	**Alcohol** none	**Milk for the Day** 1 $^1/_3$ cups skim or 1 cup lowfat
Alcohol none		**Alcohol** none

THURSDAY	FRIDAY	SATURDAY	SUNDAY
Breakfast Hedgerow yogurt (p. 49)	**Breakfast** Banana and straw- berry smoothie (p. 48)	**Breakfast** Hedgerow yogurt (p. 49)	**Breakfast** Spiced tomato and bacon toasts (p. 50) and fresh fruit
Mid-morning snack Prune and hazelnut "salami" (p. 65)	**Mid-morning snack** 2 Soft hazelnut chews (p. 58)	**Mid-morning snack** Banana-sicle (p. 58)	**Mid-morning snack** Warm popcorn (p. 70)
Lunch Beet, potato, and apple salad (p. 83) **Dessert** Lowfat yogurt and a pear	**Lunch** Vegetable soup (p. 79) **Dessert** Strawberry tart (p. 137)	**Lunch** Indonesian jumbo shrimp curry (p. 88) **Dessert** Seared pineapple with pomegranate salsa (p. 134)	**Lunch** Panzanella salad (p. 79) **Dessert** Basmati rice pudding (p. 140)
Mid-afternoon 4 Mini seed snacks (p. 62)	**Mid-afternoon** Oat thin (p. 58) and milky drink ($2/3$ cup lowfat milk)	**Mid-afternoon** Spiced seed mix (p. 61) with dish of lowfat yogurt	**Mid-afternoon** Apricot mug loaf, 1 slice (p. 68)
Dinner White bean and lamb stew (p. 109) **Dessert** Summer berry fruit jello (p. 130)	**Dinner** Noodles with chicken, shrimp, squid (p. 121) **Dessert** Papaya and lime sherbet (p. 133)	**Dinner** Spaghetti with zucchini, ricotta, basil, and lemon (p. 101) **Dessert** Stovetop plums (p. 138)	**Dinner** Sunday pot roast (p. 124) **Dessert** Anna's iced berry crush (p. 133)
	Bedtime Hot chocolate nightcap (p. 73)		**Bedtime** Hot chocolate nightcap (p. 73)
Milk for the Day $1^1/3$ cups skim or 1 cup lowfat	**Milk for the Day** $1^1/3$ cups skim or 1 cup lowfat	**Milk for the Day** $1^1/3$ cups skim or 1 cup lowfat	**Milk for the Day** $1^1/3$ cups skim or 1 cup lowfat
Alcohol none	**Alcohol** 6 ounces wine + sparkling water	**Alcohol** 1 shot (2 tablespoons) liquor & low-cal mixer	**Alcohol** 1 shot liquor + low-cal mixer

Weight maintenance plan

MONDAY

Breakfast
Quick avocado sandwich (p. 49) and fresh fruit

Mid-morning snack
Indian-style cottage cheese (p. 67) with red pepper sticks

Lunch
More than a mouthful tomato soup (p. 95)
Dessert
Mango fool (p. 140)

Mid-afternoon
Banana loaf (p. 73)

Dinner
Tuna, pink grapefruit, and avocado salad (p. 114)
Dessert
Basmati rice pudding (p. 140)

Evening snack
Hot chocolate nightcap (p. 73)

Milk for the Day
As before

Alcohol
2 units

TUESDAY

Breakfast
Super slices (p. 50) with fresh fruit

Mid-morning snack
Date and rhubarb cake wedge (p. 68)

Lunch
Spicy bean baked potato (p. 89)
Dessert
Spiced seed mix (p. 61) and $2/3$ cup fat-free fromage frais

Mid-afternoon
Roasted soybeans (p. 70) and a small glass of fresh fruit juice

Dinner
Tomato, tofu cocktail (p. 61)
Penne with artichokes (p. 100)
Dessert
Pears in nightshirts (p. 134)

Evening snack
Hot chocolate nightcap (p. 73)

Milk for the Day
As before

Alcohol
none

WEDNESDAY

Breakfast
Mother grain pudding (p. 48) with 1 slice bread (p. 49)

Mid-morning snack
Soft cheese dip with apple (p. 65)

Lunch
Avocado dip and tomato wedges (p. 90)
Dessert
Strawberry tart (p. 137)

Mid-afternoon
Date and tahini dip (p. 65)

Dinner
Asian meatballs (p. 127)
Dessert
Fresh figs with rosewater foam gratin (p. 137)

Evening snack
2 Mini seed snacks (p. 62)
Hot chocolate nightcap (p. 73)

Milk for the Day
As before

Alcohol
2 units

THURSDAY	FRIDAY	SATURDAY	SUNDAY
Breakfast Hedgerow yogurt (p. 49) with 1 slice oat, soy, and linseed bread (p. 49)	**Breakfast** Mediterranean breakfast plate (p. 54)	**Breakfast** Boiled eggs with asparagus "soldiers" (p. 53)	**Breakfast** Mushrooms on toast (p. 54) with fresh fruit
Mid-morning snack Shrimp salad (p. 66)	**Mid-morning snack** 2 graham cracker cookies (p. 61)	**Mid-morning snack** Apricot mug loaf, 1 slice (p. 68)	**Mid-morning snack** Spiced seed mix (p. 61) and $2/3$ cup lowfat yogurt
Lunch Mixed grain, seed, and herb salad (p. 93) **Dessert** 1 cup blueberries and $2/3$ cup fatfree fromage frais	**Lunch** Asian chicken and lettuce rolls (p. 95) **Dessert** Stovetop plums (p. 138)	**Lunch** Cauliflower rarebit (p. 90) **Dessert** Afghan cardamom puddings (p. 133)	**Lunch** Low-GI pizza (p. 93) **Dessert** Fresh figs with rosewater foam gratin (p. 137)
Mid-afternoon Red lentil bar (p. 71)	**Mid-afternoon** Prune and hazelnut "salami" (p. 65)	**Mid-afternoon** Spiced seed mix (p. 61) and dish of lowfat yogurt	**Mid-afternoon** Apricot and pistachio "salami" (p. 65) and a small glass of fresh fruit juice
Dinner Trout in a pea and artichoke stew (p. 113) **Dessert** Bacoffee pots (p. 140)	**Dinner** Poached salmon and tahini sauce (p. 116) **Dessert** Basmati rice pudding (p. 140)	**Dinner** Broiled chicken with spinach and lentils (p. 118) **Dessert** Apple galette (p. 138)	**Dinner** Venison cutlets (p. 122) **Dessert** Roasted peaches with blueberries (p. 138)
Evening snack 4 graham cracker cookies (p. 61)	**Evening snack** 2 Oat thins (p. 58)	**Evening snack** 2 Soft hazelnut chews (p. 58)	**Evening snack** Hot chocolate nightcap (p. 73)
Milk for the Day As before	**Milk for the Day** As before	**Milk for the Day** As before	**Milk for the Day** As before
Alcohol 2 units	**Alcohol** 2 units	**Alcohol** 2 units	**Alcohol** none

breakfast

This meal is crucial for your blood glucose levels and will set you up for the day. It is also a great opportunity to eat one or two portions of fruit and veg, and our recipes will help you do this. We have also included a recipe for an oat, soy, and linseed bread that is specified in other recipes – but where we have listed a soy and linseed bread, we suggest using Vogel – as photographed here.

banana and cinnamon oatmeal

A sustaining twist on a classic favorite. Leftovers will keep in the fridge for 1-2 days; reheat the oatmeal with a little extra water, either in the microwave or on the stove.

SERVES 6

- 2 cups rolled oats with oatbran
- ½ teaspoon ground cinnamon
- 4 medium bananas
- 2 tablespoons honey
- 3 cups strawberries, hulled and cut in half

1 Bring 4 cups water to a boil in a large saucepan, then pour in the oats, stirring all the time until well mixed. Stir in the cinnamon.

2 Bring to a simmer, then simmer gently for about 10 minutes, adding extra water if you want to give a soft consistency. Stir occasionally.

3 Roughly mash three of the bananas and stir them through the oatmeal. Remove from the heat and stir in the honey.

4 Slice the remaining banana and mix with the strawberries. Spoon the oatmeal into bowls and serve at once, topped with the fruit.

PER SERVING: 221 calories; 3g fat; 0.5g saturated fat; 45g carbohydrate; 0.01g sodium

tropical fruit tabbouleh

Tabbouleh is made with bulgur or cracked wheat and is normally a savory salad with loads of parsley, mint, garlic, and tomatoes, but for those wanting a sweet version that ticks the healthy eating boxes, give this one a go! It is best to make this the night before as it needs a couple of hours to soak and rest, but it will keep, covered, in the fridge for 3-4 days.

SERVES 4

- 2 tablespoons light brown sugar
- 4 cardamom pods, lightly crushed
- 1 small bunch mint
- pulp from 4 passion fruits
- finely grated zest and juice of 2 limes
- 1 cup bulgur or cracked wheat
- 1 cup peeled pineapple, cut up
- 1 kiwi fruit, cut up
- 1 pomegranate, peeled and seeds separated
- 1 small banana, thinly sliced
- 1 papaya, seeded and cut up

1 Put the sugar in a small saucepan with 1½ cups water, the cardamom pods, half the mint, all the passion fruit pulp, and the lime zest. Bring slowly to a boil, then simmer gently for 5 minutes.

2 Put the bulgur in a large bowl and strain the hot syrup over it, squeezing out all the juice from the pulp left in the strainer. Cover and let it sit for up to 1 hour, until the grains have swelled and absorbed all the liquid.

3 Pick the reserved mint leaves from the stalks and chop them finely. Stir into the bulgur along with the lime juice and all the prepared fruit. Cover and let the flavours develop for 1 hour if possible.

PER SERVING: 249 calories; 1g fat; 0.1g saturated fat; 58g carbohydrate; 0.01g sodium

citrus fruit salad

Goji berries, oval red berries grown in China, are considered to be one of the most nutritionally rich fruits available. Dried goji berries are available in health food stores.

SERVES 2

- 2 pink or red grapefruit
- 2 oranges
- 4 clementines (or tangerines)
- 2 tablespoons golden raisins
- 1½ cups lowfat plain yogurt

1 Using a small serrated knife, peel the grapefruit and oranges, removing all the white pith. Squeeze any juice from the trimmings and reserve.
2 Carefully remove the segments of fruit from the membrane that holds them in place. Squeeze the trimmings once more to collect all the juice.
3 Peel the clementines and cut horizontally in thin slices. Mix all the fruits with the reserved juices and the goji berries, or raisins, and serve with the yogurt.

PER SERVING: 237 calories; 2g fat; 1g saturated fat; 47g carbohydrate; 0.13g sodium

asian eggs

Something a little different for breakfast, quick to make and satisfying to eat. As this recipe is low in carbohydrate, make sure you have a carb-rich snack before lunch – the dill and buttermilk roll on page 66 would be perfect or a slice or two of seeded bread with a little reduced-calorie jam.

SERVES 4

- 1 teaspoon canola oil
- 1 teaspoon sesame oil
- ½ red pepper, cut in ½-inch squares
- 2 scallions, sliced
- ½ cup mushrooms, quartered
- ½ cup bean sprouts, rinsed and dried
- 6 medium eggs
- 2 teaspoons fish sauce (nam pla)
- 1 teaspoon reduced-salt soy sauce
- freshly ground white pepper
- 4 slices soy and linseed bread, toasted (see page 49)

1 Heat the oils in a nonstick frying pan or wok over medium heat and cook the red pepper, scallions, and mushrooms for about 2 minutes until softening, then add the bean sprouts and cook for another 1 minute.
2 Meanwhile, beat the eggs with the fish sauce, soy sauce, and a little pepper, then pour the eggs over the vegetables and stir, drawing the sides in as you would for scrambled eggs until the eggs are set to your liking.
3 Serve immediately, with the toast.

PER SERVING: 245 calories; 13g fat; 3g saturated fat; 18g carbohydrate; 0.66g sodium

mother grain pudding
with sunshine fruits

Quinoa (pronounced keen-wah) was one of the most sacred foods of the Incas – they called it "mother grain" because of its nutritious qualities (though it's a seed rather than a grain). It can be used in both sweet and savory dishes. This pudding will keep in the fridge for 2-3 days.

SERVES 4

- ¾ cup quinoa
- 1 cup fat-free plain yogurt
- ⅔ cup lowfat milk
- 1 tablespoon honey
- 1 large papaya
- 1 large mango
- 4 passion fruits

1 Rinse the quinoa well in a fine mesh strainer under running cold water, then tip it into a pan of 1¼ cups of boiling water. Stir well, then cover and simmer for 10 minutes.
2 Remove from the heat and let it go cold. Put the quinoa in a bowl and loosen the "grains" with a fork. Stir in the yogurt, milk, and honey.
3 Prepare the papaya and mango and cut in bite-size pieces. Cut the passion fruits in half, remove the seeds and pulp, and combine them with the papaya and mango.
4 Spoon the pudding into bowls and top with the fruit.

PER SERVING: 228 calories; 3g fat; 0.5g saturated fat; 44g carbohydrate; 0.09g sodium

banana and
strawberry smoothie

Try to choose locally grown strawberries wherever possible – they will have so much more flavor than imported ones.

SERVES 2

- 2 large bananas
- 1 cup strawberries, hulled
- 2 tablespoons fat-free plain yogurt
- 1 cup milk
- 1 tablespoon honey
- 1 tablespoon wheat germ
- 12 ice cubes

Place all the ingredients in a blender and blend until smooth. Serve at once.

PER SERVING: 228 calories; 3g fat; 1g saturated fat; 46g carbohydrate; 0.06g sodium

oat, soy, and linseed bread

This dense loaf freezes well, but slice it first.

MAKES 18 SLICES

- 2 cups rolled oats
- ⅓ cup soybeans, coarsely ground
- 2 cups whole-wheat flour with malted wheat berries
- 1 envelope (6–7g) rapid-rise (fast-action) yeast
- 1 teaspoon salt
- 2 tablespoons linseeds
- 1 teaspoon canola oil, to grease a 2-pound loaf pan

1 Mix the oats with 1 cup cold water. Cover and let soak for at least 2 hours.

2 Combine the remaining ingredients and add to the soaked oats with about ⅔ cup lukewarm water. Mix to a firm, but not sticky dough. Turn out onto a lightly floured surface and knead for 2 minutes.

3 Shape to fit the prepared loaf pan and press down gently. Cover loosely with a plastic bag and leave in a warm place to rise for 2–3 hours until the dough has reached the top of the pan and has a slightly domed surface.

5 Preheat the oven to 425°F and bake for 45 mins until the loaf is risen and firm and sounds hollow when tapped on the bottom. Cool on a wire rack.

PER SLICE: 105 calories; 2g fat; 0.3g saturated fat; 17g carbohydrate; 0.11g sodium

SERVING SUGGESTION

Banana sandwich – mash half a small banana and sandwich it between 2 slices.
Avocado sandwich – mash a quarter of a ripe medium avocado with a teaspoon of Worcestershire sauce between 2 slices of bread.

BANANA SANDWICH - PER SERVING: 246 cals; 4g fat; 1g saturated fat; 43g carbohydrate; 0.22g sodium

AVOCADO SANDWICH - PER SERVING: 330 cals; 16g fat; 2g saturated fat; 36g carbohydrate; 0.28g sodium

hedgerow yogurt

Whole wheat "berries" and spelt grains are available in health food stores. Soak them overnight, then drain and cook in fresh boiling water for 30-35 minutes until tender. Drain and use in salads or in this fruity mixture. This yogurt will keep in the fridge for 1-2 days.

SERVES 2

- ½ vanilla bean, split
- 1½ cups fat-free yogurt
- 2 cups blackberries
- 2 dessert apples, cored and grated
- ⅓ cup cooked wheat berries or spelt grains

Scrape the seeds from the vanilla bean and mix with the yogurt. Fold in the blackberries, grated apple, and wheat berries, and serve.

PER SERVING: 251 calories; 1g fat; 0.1g saturated fat; 44g carbohydrate; 0.12g sodium

super slices

Perfect for a quick breakfast – do have the yogurt and apple as well. If you don't trust yourself to limit the portion, then store in an airtight container in the freezer!

SERVES 6

- ⅓ cup dried dates, chopped
- ½ cup whole-wheat flour with malted wheat berries
- 2 teaspoons baking powder
- 2 teaspoons ground apple pie spice (or pumpkin pie spice)
- 6 ready-to-eat dried apricots, chopped
- ½ cup chopped walnut pieces
- 3 tablespoons sunflower seeds
- ⅓ cup citrons (candied peel), rinsed and dried
- 1 egg, beaten with 4 tablespoons lowfat milk
- 4 cups lowfat plain yogurt
- 6 small dessert apples

1 Preheat the oven to 350°F. Line the bottom and sides of a 1-pound loaf pan with baking paper.
2 Put the dates in a small saucepan with ¼ cup water and simmer for about 5 minutes until softened. Let cool.
3 Mix the flour, baking powder, and spice in a large bowl, then stir in the rest of the dry ingredients. Add the cooled date puree, and the egg and milk and mix until evenly combined.
4 Transfer to the prepared pan and level the surface. Bake for about 35 minutes until risen and firm to the touch. Cool slightly, then remove from the pan and let cool on a wire rack. When cold, cut into 6 thick chunks (or 12 for 2 slices per portion, or 18 for 3 slices per portion – thin slices), and serve each portion with ⅔ cup yogurt and an apple.

PER SERVING: 332 calories; 11g fat; 2g saturated fat; 47g carbohydrate; 0.37g sodium

spiced broiled tomato and bacon toasts

Spice up your breakfast a little with these indulgent tomatoes, but make sure you eat a large orange as well to get a good range of nutrients.

SERVES 4

- 8 plum tomatoes, cut in half lengthwise
- 1 teaspoon light brown sugar
- 2 teaspoons mild or medium-hot curry powder
- ¼ teaspoon freshly ground black pepper
- 2 teaspoons olive oil
- 3 ounces lean bacon, diced
- 4 slices soy and linseed bread, toasted (see page 49)
- 4 large oranges, as an accompaniment

1 Preheat the broiler to high. Arrange the tomato halves, cut-side up, on a baking tray. Mix together the sugar, curry powder, and pepper, and sprinkle it over the cut surface of the tomatoes.
2 Drizzle each tomato half with a few drops of oil, then broil for 8-10 minutes until the tomatoes are soft but not collapsed.
3 Sprinkle the chopped bacon over the tomatoes and return to the broiler for 2-3 minutes.
4 Put four halves of tomatoes on each slice of toast and serve immediately.

PER SERVING: 244 calories; 6g fat; 1g saturated fat; 37g carbohydrate; 0.56g sodium

boiled eggs
with asparagus "soldiers"

In England, strips of toast served with soft-boiled eggs are called "soldiers," and this is my version of that classic recipe. Not for every day as it is higher in calories than the other breakfasts in this chapter, but perfect for a special treat!

SERVES 1

- ½ pound bundle asparagus, trimmed (about 6 ounces trimmed weight)
- 2 medium eggs
- freshly ground black pepper or smoked paprika, for sprinkling
- 2 slices oat, soy, and linseed bread (see page 49), for serving

1 Steam or cook the asparagus in boiling water for 5-7 minutes, depending on the thickness of the stalks. The stalks should be tender but still with a "bite" (al dente). Drain thoroughly.

2 Meanwhile, cook the eggs in simmering water for 3-5 minutes depending on your personal preference: 3 minutes will give a very lightly cooked egg, 4 minutes will give a fairly firm white and a runny yolk, 5 minutes will give a firm white and a lightly cooked yolk.

3 Serve the eggs and asparagus at once, with ground black pepper or smoked paprika sprinkled over them, and the bread cut into "soldiers."

PER SERVING: 398 calories; 16g fat; 4g saturated fat; 38g carbohydrate; 0.31g sodium

roast tomatoes
with field
mushrooms and chickpeas

A dish that can be prepped in advance and popped in the oven when you are ready to eat. Serve with a glass of fresh orange juice.

SERVES 2

- 4 large tomatoes
- 1 tablespoon extra virgin olive oil
- 1 garlic clove, finely chopped
- ½ small onion, finely chopped
- ½ pound mushrooms, roughly chopped
- 4 tablespoons canned chickpeas, rinsed
- 1 teaspoon fresh thyme leaves, finely chopped
- freshly ground black pepper, to taste
- 2 slices whole-wheat bread, toasted

1 Slice off the top of each tomato, about ½ inch down, and set aside. With a teaspoon, paring knife, or melon baller, scoop out the seeds and central core of the tomato, being careful not to split the sides of the tomato. Discard the seeds.

2 Heat the olive oil in a frying pan, then add the garlic and onion and cook over a low heat until the onions have softened but not colored. Remove the onions and garlic and set aside.

3 In the same frying pan, cook the mushrooms over a high heat until they have started to wilt. Stir in the onion mixture and the chickpeas, and season with thyme and black pepper.

4 Preheat the oven to 400ºF. Fill the tomato cases with the mushroom mixture and replace the tops of the tomatoes. Set the 4 tomatoes on a roasting tray and cook in the oven until the tomatoes have softened but not split (about 15-20 minutes). Serve immediately, with the toast and orange juice.

PER SERVING INCLUDING JUICE: 284 calories; 9g fat; 1g saturated fat; 43g carbohydrate; 0.24g sodium

mushrooms on toast

This is great for brunch or breakfast; the flavors of each part of the dish really come together.

SERVES 2

- 1 teaspoon sesame oil
- 1 garlic clove, crushed
- 1 green chile, seeded and finely chopped
- 1¼-inch piece of fresh ginger, peeled and grated
- 12 ounces button mushrooms, cut in half
- 1 tablespoon reduced-salt soy sauce
- 1 teaspoon honey
- 2 heads bok choy, shredded
- 4 scallions, sliced
- 1 tablespoon sesame seeds
- freshly ground black pepper
- 4 slices oat, soy, and linseed bread (see page 49), toasted, for serving

1 Heat the sesame oil in a large nonstick frying pan. Add the garlic, chile, and ginger, and cook for 30 seconds, stirring constantly.
2 Add the mushrooms and cook for 2 minutes, stirring from time to time, until lightly golden.
3 Stir in the soy sauce, honey, bok choy, and scallions and cook for another 3 minutes, stirring occasionally. Add a splash of water if necessary to prevent sticking. Stir in the sesame seeds and season with black pepper.
4 Serve immediately, with the toast.

PER SERVING: 330 calories; 11g fat; 2g saturated fat; 43g carbohydrate; 0.80g sodium

mediterranean breakfast plate

Throughout much of the southern Mediterranean you may see this on the breakfast menu. Make sure the tomatoes are at room temperature for the best flavor.

SERVES 3

- 4 large tomatoes, cut in wedges
- 7 ounces cucumber, cut in chunks
- 5 ounces reduced-fat feta-style cheese, cut in thin slices
- 9 black olives
- 2 teaspoons olive oil
- freshly chopped marjoram, for sprinkling
- freshly ground black pepper, for sprinkling
- 6 slices oat, soy, and linseed bread (see page 49), for serving

Arrange the tomatoes, cucumber, cheese, and olives on three plates. Sprinkle with olive oil, marjoram, and pepper, and serve with the bread.

PER SERVING: 355 calories; 13g fat; 4g saturated fat; 41g carbohydrate; 1.04g sodium

snacks

These healthy snacks are perfect to bridge the gaps between meals – there's even a luxurious hot chocolate to enjoy just before bedtime. Make up a batch of a couple of recipes so you will have a variety on hand, but be sure not to eat them all in one go.

soft hazelnut chews

These lovely bites make a great afternoon snack.

MAKES 12 CHEWS
- ¾ cup shelled hazelnuts
- ¼ cup light brown sugar
- ½ teaspoon natural vanilla extract
- 2 egg whites

1 Preheat the oven to 350°F. Put the hazelnuts on a baking tray and roast to a golden brown color – about 15 minutes. Increase the oven temperature to 400°F. Line a baking tray with baking paper.
2 Put the nuts and sugar in a food processor and pulse, then add the vanilla and 1 of the egg whites and pulse to a paste.
3 Whisk the remaining egg white until stiff and fold the nut mixture into it. Scoop 12 spoonfuls onto the baking tray, allowing room between, and spread each one a little. Bake for 10-15 minutes until golden.
4 Let cool a little, then transfer to a wire rack until cold. Store in an airtight container. Freeze, if you prefer.

PER SERVING: 70 calories; 5g fat; 0.4g saturated fat; 4g carbohydrate; 0.01g sodium

oat thins

These crisp cookies are almost irresistible, so store these in the freezer, then you can get ONE out as a snack either mid-morning or afternoon.

MAKES 12 THINS
- 1 cup rolled oats
- ⅓ cup unrefined light brown sugar
- 2 tablespoons whole-wheat flour with malted wheat berries
- 2 egg whites, lightly beaten
- 2 tablespoons unsalted butter, melted

1 Preheat the oven to 375°F. Line a large baking tray with baking paper.
2 Mix all the ingredients together. Drop 12 spoonfuls, well spaced, onto the baking tray, then, using a fork, flatten each one to about 3½ inches wide.
3 Bake for 15-20 minutes until golden brown. Let cool on the tray, then transfer to a wire rack until cold and crisp. Store in an airtight container. Freeze, if you prefer.

PER SERVING (ONE COOKIE): 81 calories; 3g fat; 1g saturated fat; 13g carbohydrate; 0.01g sodium

banana-sicles

The simplest recipe to make, but a delicious snack to have in the freezer.

SERVES 4
- 2 large bananas

Peel each banana and cut in half crosswise. Push a popsicle stick into the cut end, then wrap in plastic wrap and freeze until required.

PER SERVING: 71 calories; 0.2g fat; 0.1g saturated fat; 17g carbohydrate; 0g sodium

spiced seed mix

A portion of these, with a glass of water, will stave off hunger pangs. Measure out each portion separately so you don't over-indulge.

SERVES 12
- ½ cup pumpkin seeds
- ½ cup sunflower seeds
- 1 teaspoon reduced-salt soy sauce
- ¼ teaspoon chili powder

1 Preheat the oven to 375°F.
2 Mix all the ingredients together and transfer to a baking tray.
3 Bake for 10 minutes until dried and lightly golden. Let cool, then store in an airtight container, either in the fridge or the freezer.

PER SERVING: 72 calories; 6g fat; 1g saturated fat; 2g carbohydrate; 0.02g sodium

tomato tofu cocktail

SERVES 2
- 14½-ounce can chopped tomatoes
- 1 x 4-ounce cake silken tofu
- juice of ½ lime
- 1 tablespoon Worcestershire sauce, or more to taste
- ½ teaspoon hot pepper sauce
- 4 ice cubes
- celery stalks, for serving

1 Put the canned tomatoes into a blender, then add half a can of cold water and the remaining ingredients.
2 Whizz until smooth, then serve with the celery.

PER SERVING: 75 calories; 3g fat; 0.3g saturated fat; 7g carbohydrate; 0.31g sodium

"graham cracker" cookies

You can also bake these in muffin cups to make a cookie-like case for a spoonful of fromage frais and fruit.

MAKES 14 COOKIES
- 1 cup medium oatmeal
- ¾ cup whole-wheat flour with malted wheat berries
- 2 tablespoons light brown sugar
- 1 teaspoon baking powder
- 2 tablespoons canola oil
- 4 tablespoons milk

1 Preheat the oven to 375°F.
2 Combine the dry ingredients in a bowl (or a food processor) and mix in the oil and milk to make a firm dough. (If it feels a little too dry to roll out, add a few drops of water.)
3 Roll the dough, as thinly as possible, between two layers of plastic wrap. Use a 3½-inch-wide cookie cutter to press out your cookies, and transfer them to a nonstick baking tray. Dampen and re-roll the trimmings as necessary.
4 Bake for about 15 minutes until lightly golden. Let them go cold on a wire rack, then store in an airtight container.

PER SERVING: 75 calories; 2g fat; 0.4g saturated fat; 12g carbohydrate; 0.05g sodium

mini seed snacks

These savory crackers contain a great mix of seeds – the linseed, pumpkin, and sesame seeds are a good plant source of omega 3 fatty acids and they will also provide beneficial phytoestrogens.

MAKES 30 CRACKERS (2 PER PORTION)

- **2 tablespoons pumpkin seeds**
- **1 tablespoon sunflower seeds**
- **1 tablespoon linseeds**
- **1 tablespoon sesame seeds**
- **1½ cups whole-wheat flour with malted wheat berries**
- **½ teaspoon rapid-rise (fast action) yeast**
- **½ teaspoon yeast extract (e.g., Marmite or Vegemite) mixed with 1 teaspoon boiling water**
- **2 tablespoons finely grated Parmesan cheese**

1 Preheat the oven to 400°F. Lightly oil a 10 x 12-inch cookie sheet.

2 Combine all the seeds in a bowl and mix well. Put the flour, yeast, and half the seeds in a food processor and mix to a firm dough with ⅔ cup lukewarm water. Knead lightly, then roll out thinly between two sheets of waxed paper.

3 Lay the sheet of dough onto the cookie sheet and brush with the yeast extract. Press the remaining seeds on top and sprinkle with the cheese.

4 Bake for 10 minutes until lightly golden, then carefully transfer onto a cutting board. Reduce the temperature to 325°F, cut the dough into 30 pieces and return to the oven for 15-20 minutes until fairly crisp and golden.

5 Let cool on a wire rack until completely cold and crisp. Store in an airtight container.

PER SERVING: 66 calories; 2g fat; 0.4g saturated fat; 10g carbohydrate; 0.02g sodium

grilled zucchini
with lime and mint

Delicious warm or cold, this is more satisfying than a cookie, but only 40 calories. They are also a great way to bump up your veg intake.

SERVES 4

- **olive oil, for spraying/greasing**
- **4 large zucchini**
- **4 tablespoons chopped mint leaves**
- **freshly ground black pepper**
- **2 limes, cut in half**

1 Preheat a nonstick ridged grill pan over a high heat. When ready to cook, spray it very lightly with olive oil.

2 Trim and cut each zucchini lengthwise into 8 slices. Lay the slices, in batches, on the grill pan and cook for 2-3 minutes each side until softened and marked with the ridges. Turn and cook on the other side.

3 Serve sprinkled with mint and pepper, and squeeze the lime halves over them.

PER SERVING: 40 calories; 1g fat; 0.2g saturated fat; 4g carbohydrate; 0g sodium

prune and hazelnut "salami"

There's no meat in this fruity snack, but it is shaped like a salami. Toast the nuts in the oven at 375°F for about 15 minutes, or chop them first, then toast them in a dry frying pan over medium heat. This "salami" will keep in the fridge for up to 1 month.

SERVES 6

- 2 cups ready-to-eat prunes
- ¼ teaspoon ground star anise
- 1 teaspoon finely grated orange zest
- 1 teaspoon sesame seeds
- 3 tablespoons shelled hazelnuts, toasted and chopped

1 Roughly chop the prunes (you can do this in the food processor), then mix well with the remaining ingredients.
2 Transfer to a piece of plastic wrap and shape into a "log," twisting the ends of the plastic wrap tightly. Store in the fridge until required.
3 Cut a portion in slices as a quick snack straight from the fridge.

PER SERVING: 92 calories; 3g fat; 0.3g saturated fat; 15g carbohydrate; 0.01g sodium

VARIATION For an Apricot and Pistachio variation, simply replace the prunes with dried apricots and the hazelnuts with pistachios.

PER SERVING: 98 calories; 3g fat; 0.3g saturated fat; 16g carbohydrate; 0.01g sodium

soft cheese and orange dip

The citrus zest balances the richness of the cheese and dates in this unusual dip.

SERVES 4

- 1½ ounces pitted dates (about 6-7), chopped
- finely grated zest and juice of 1 orange
- ½ cup light cream cheese
- 2 dessert apples, cored and thinly sliced

1 Put the dates and orange juice in a small saucepan and heat gently just until softened. Let them go cold, then beat in the zest and cheese.
2 Serve with the apple slices as dippers.

PER SERVING: 99 calories; 3g fat; 2g saturated fat; 16g carbohydrate; 0.1g sodium

date and tahini dip

This is a Middle Eastern variation of the cheese and orange dip above.

SERVES 4

- 2½ ounces pitted dates (about 12-13), chopped
- finely grated zest and juice of 1 lemon
- 1 tablespoon tahini
- 2 medium pears, quartered, cored and thinly sliced

1 Put the dates in a small saucepan with the lemon juice and cook over a gentle heat just until the dates are softened, adding a dash of water if necessary. Cool, then stir in the lemon zest and tahini.
2 Serve with pear slices for dipping.

PER SERVING: 101 calories; 2g fat; 0.3g saturated fat; 20g carbohydrate; 0.01g sodium

shrimp salad
with herb dip

A classic recipe but with a lot less fat – I've used
fat-free yogurt here instead of mayonnaise.

SERVES 2

- ½ pound cooked shrimp in their shell,
  rinsed and dried
- ⅔ cup no-fat yogurt
- 1 garlic clove, crushed
- 1 tablespoon chopped cilantro
- 2 teaspoons chopped mint leaves
- ¼ teaspoon freshly ground black pepper

1 Pile the shrimp into a tumbler and chill in the
fridge until needed.
2 Mix together the remaining ingredients, cover,
and ideally leave for at least 1 hour for the flavors
to develop.
3 Serve the dip with the shrimp, peeling them at
the table.

PER SERVING: 86 calories; 0.4g fat; 0.1g saturated fat;
4g carbohydrate; 0.33g sodium

dill and
buttermilk rolls

Frozen rolls can be thawed and refreshed one at
a time in the microwave. To prepare one of these
from frozen, set it on a piece of paper towel and
microwave on high heat for 20–30 seconds only.

MAKES 18 ROLLS

- 3¾ cups whole-wheat flour with malted
  wheat berries
- ⅔ ounce fresh dill, finely chopped
- 1½ teaspoons baking soda
- 1 cup buttermilk
- about ⅔ cup lowfat milk

1 Preheat the oven to 450°F. Sprinkle a baking
tray with flour.
2 In a large mixing bowl, stir together the flour,
dill, and baking soda. Make a well in the center
and add the buttermilk and half the milk.
3 Mix to a soft yet not sticky dough, adding
extra milk as necessary, then transfer to a lightly
floured surface and shape into a ball.
4 Cut the dough into 18 equal pieces and roughly
shape each one into a roll. Set on the prepared
baking tray and bake for about 20 minutes until
risen and crusty and hollow-sounding when
tapped on the bottom.
5 Cool on a wire tray. Store in an airtight
container. Freeze, if you prefer.

PER SERVING: 98 calories; 1g fat; 0.2g saturated fat;
21g carbohydrate; 0.13g sodium

Indian-style cottage cheese

Scoop up this delicious dip with some romaine or Belgian endive leaves.

SERVES 2

- ½ teaspoon cumin seeds
- ½ cup finely chopped red onion
- 1 medium-sized red chile, seeded and finely chopped
- 2 tablespoons chopped cilantro
- ½ cup reduced-fat cottage cheese

1 Dry-fry the cumin seeds in a small frying pan over a medium heat just until they smell fragrant.
2 Combine all the ingredients and mix well. Serve with romaine or Belgian endive leaves as suggested to scoop up the dip.

PER SERVING: 98 calories; 2g fat; 0g saturated fat; 6g carbohydrate; 0.3g sodium

chili bean pâté

Use chunks of raw vegetables as dippers – I like cucumber, celery, or carrots.

SERVES 4

- 1 teaspoon olive oil
- 1 shallot, finely chopped
- 1 garlic clove, finely chopped
- 1½ teaspoons ground cumin
- 1½ teaspoons ground coriander
- ½ teaspoon chili powder
- 1 x 15-ounce can kidney beans in water, drained and rinsed
- juice of ½ lime, or more to taste

1 Heat the oil in a small frying pan and sauté the shallot and garlic until softened. Stir in the spices and cook, stirring over a gentle heat, for 30 seconds.
2 Put the beans, spice mixture, and lime juice in a food processor and pulse to a chunky texture, adding 1-2 tablespoons water, as required. Add extra lime juice to suit taste.
3 Serve with chunks of vegetables as suggested.

PER SERVING: 90 calories; 2g fat; 0.1g saturated fat; 14g carbohydrate; 0.28g sodium

date and rhubarb cake wedges

This cake has a sweet and chewy texture. The dates and rhubarb keep it moist, so it will also freeze well (cut it into wedges first so that you can defrost a piece at a time).

SERVES 12

- 1⅓ cups pitted dates, chopped
- 6½ ounces rhubarb, chopped
- ⅓ cup plus 1 tablespoon unsalted butter
- 1½ cups minus 1 tablespoon whole-wheat flour with malted wheat berries
- 1 tablespoon baking powder
- 3 medium eggs, beaten
- 1½ teaspoons vanilla extract

1 Preheat the oven to 350°F. Line the bottom of a 9-inch round cake pan with baking paper and spray the sides very lightly with oil.
2 Put the dates in a small saucepan, add the rhubarb and 6 tablespoons cold water, then cover and simmer, stirring occasionally, until softened to a rough puree. Beat in the butter and let it cool.
3 Put the flour in a mixing bowl, add the baking powder, date mixture, eggs, and vanilla extract, and mix well.
4 Transfer to the prepared pan and level the surface. Bake for about 25 minutes until risen and just firm to the touch.
5 Cool on a wire rack. Store in an airtight container.

PER SERVING: 96 calories; 5g fat; 3g saturated fat; 12g carbohydrate; 0.16g sodium

apricot mug loaf

You don't even need scales for this one – all the measurements are based on a coffee mug. This loaf also freezes well.

MAKES 16 SLICES

- 1 mug high-fiber bran cereal
- ⅓ mug dark brown sugar
- 1 mug ready-to-eat dried apricots, chopped
- 1 mug lowfat milk
- 1 mug whole-wheat flour with malted wheat berries
- 1 tablespoon baking powder
- 1 tablespoon caraway seeds (optional)

1 Put the cereal in a bowl, mix in the sugar, apricots, and milk, then cover and let soak for 2 hours or thereabouts.
2 Preheat the oven to 350°F. Line a 2-pound loaf pan with baking paper.
3 Add the flour, baking powder, and caraway seeds, if using, to the soaked cereal and beat well until evenly mixed. Transfer the mixture to the prepared pan and level the surface.
4 Bake for about 50 minutes until risen and firm to the touch. Cool in the pan, then transfer to a wire rack until completely cold. Wrap in kitchen foil and store in an airtight container, or freeze in slices.

PER SERVING: 92 calories; 1g fat; 0.3g saturated fat; 20g carbohydrate; 0.17g sodium

roasted soy beans

You can experiment with other seeds and herbs as you choose.

SERVES 8

- **1¼ cups soybeans**
- **4-6 sprigs of fresh rosemary**
- **1 teaspoon fennel seeds**
- **1 teaspoon cumin seeds**
- **freshly ground black pepper**

1 Soak the beans in cold water overnight. Drain and rinse. Transfer to a large saucepan and cover with boiling water. Return to a boil, then simmer for 10 minutes. Drain thoroughly.

2 Preheat the oven to 400°F. Line two baking trays with sheets of baking paper or lightly grease them with oil.

3 Divide the beans in half and pour onto the trays. Add the rosemary to one tray and the seeds to the other. Season both generously with pepper, then mix well. Ensure the beans are in a single layer.

4 Roast for about 45-60 minutes, stirring occasionally, until crisp and golden. Switch off the oven and let the beans cool in the residual heat.

5 Discard the rosemary stalks – all the "needles" will be crisp and will have fallen off. Store each tray of beans in a separate airtight container.

PER SERVING: 98 calories; 5g fat; 0g saturated fat; 5g carbohydrate; 0g sodium

warm natural popcorn

It's best to cook this fresh as you want it. There's no need to add any oil to the pan. For 2 or 4 servings, use a bigger pan and more popcorn kernels.

SERVES 1

- **2½ tablespoons popcorn kernels**
- **cinnamon or pepper for sprinkling, if you like**

1 If you don't have a hot-air popcorn popper, you can pop the kernels in a pan. Put the kernels in a medium-sized saucepan over a medium-high heat. Cover with the lid and shake over the heat until you hear the corn start to "pop."

2 Reduce the heat to medium-low and leave the pan over the heat, shaking it now and then to prevent burning, until all the popping stops. Don't be tempted to lift the lid before then! Sprinkle with cinnamon or pepper, if you like, and serve at once.

PER SERVING: 88 calories; 1g fat; 0.1g saturated fat; 19g carbohydrate; 0g sodium

red lentil bars with cucumber mint yogurt

A dish that can be made in advance and reheated for a quick nibble or a light lunch. You can also freeze any that you don't want immediately.

MAKES 24 BARS (12 PORTIONS)

- 1 tablespoon olive oil
- 1 onion, finely chopped
- 1 leek, finely chopped
- 1 carrot, finely chopped
- 1 teaspoon ground cumin
- 1 teaspoon ground coriander
- ¼ teaspoon red pepper flakes
- a scant cup dried red lentils
- 1¾ cups vegetable stock
- ½ cup oatmeal
- 1 egg, beaten

FOR THE CUCUMBER MINT YOGURT

- 1 cucumber, seeded and finely chopped
- 1 garlic clove, finely chopped
- 12 mint leaves, chopped
- ⅔ cup no-fat yogurt

1 Preheat the oven to 375°F. Line a 12- x 8-inch baking tray with baking paper or lightly grease to prevent the bars from sticking.

2 To make the cucumber mint yogurt, combine all the ingredients, then cover and chill until needed, to allow the flavors to develop.

3 Heat the oil in a medium-sized saucepan and add the onion, leek, and carrot, and cook for 10 minutes over a low heat to soften but not color the vegetables. Add the cumin, coriander, and chili, and cook for another minute.

4 Add the lentils and stock and cook, uncovered, for about 20 minutes until the lentils are tender but not too mushy, and the liquid has been absorbed. Cook for up to 10 minutes more, if necessary, to achieve this. Let cool a little, then fold in the oatmeal and egg, and stir to combine.

5 Spread the mixture evenly into the prepared baking tray and bake for 30 minutes. Cut into bars and serve with the cucumber mint yogurt.

PER SERVING: 99 calories; 3g fat; 0.4g saturated fat; 13g carbohydrate; 0.09g sodium

hot chocolate nightcap

This is a real treat for you to enjoy – warm, rich, and perfect to send you to sleep. It is also much healthier than store-bought products.

SERVES 1

- **1 tablespoon cocoa powder**
- **1 teaspoon sugar**
- **½ cup lowfat milk**

1 In a small saucepan, mix the cocoa powder and sugar with 6 tablespoons cold water. Place over a medium heat and stir until it comes to a simmer.
2 Whisk in the milk until heated through. If you prefer, heat the milk separately and whisk until frothy, then stir in the chocolate mixture. Serve at once.

PER SERVING: 99 calories; 4g fat; 2g saturated fat; 13g carbohydrate; 0.06g sodium

banana loaf

So simple you can't really go wrong. The hint of spice brings a tasty warmth to this bread. Store in an airtight container or freeze in slices.

MAKES 16 SLICES

- **2 large bananas**
- **1 medium egg**
- **2 cups minus 2 tablespoons whole-wheat flour (with malted wheat berries, if available)**
- **1 tablespoon baking powder**
- **½ teaspoon ground nutmeg**
- **⅓ cup raisins or golden raisins**
- **⅓ cup shelled pecans, chopped**

1 Preheat the oven to 350°F. Line a 2-pound loaf pan with baking paper. Alternatively, grease and lightly flour the inside of the pan.
2 Puree together the bananas, egg, and ½ cup cold water.
3 Mix the remaining ingredients together in a bowl and stir in the banana puree until evenly mixed.
4 Transfer to the prepared pan and bake for 35-40 minutes, until risen and just firm to the touch. Cool slightly, then remove from the pan and set on a wire rack until completely cold.

PER SERVING: 97 calories; 3g fat; 0.3g saturated fat; 17g carbohydrate; 0.12g sodium

Most of the recipes in this chapter can be packed in Tupperware or flasks and reheated later – perfect for packed lunches.

portable
food

a chunky potato soup

The chunks of bacon in this soup will give it a lovely smoky flavor and the carrots will provide some rich color as well as lots of useful vitamins. You can freeze this soup.

SERVES 2

- 1 onion, roughly chopped
- 2 garlic cloves, finely chopped
- 2 strips bacon, chopped
- 2 celery stalks, thinly sliced
- 1 teaspoon fresh thyme leaves
- 1 bay leaf
- 2 medium carrots, sliced
- 12 ounces new potatoes, cut into ½-inch pieces
- 2½ cups fresh chicken stock, mixed with 1½ cups water
- 3 tablespoons chopped flat-leaf parsley
- 2 tablespoons no-fat yogurt
- freshly ground black pepper

1 Put the onion, garlic, and bacon in a medium-sized, nonstick saucepan and cook, covered, over a medium heat for about 8 minutes, stirring occasionally and adding a splash of water, as necessary.

2 Add the celery, thyme, bay leaf, carrots, and potatoes, and cook until the potatoes start to stick to the bottom of the pan – about 5 minutes.

3 Add the stock and bring to a boil. Simmer, covered, for about 15 minutes until the potatoes are tender and starting to fall apart.

4 Stir in the parsley and yogurt. Season to taste with black pepper.

PER SERVING: 292 calories; 8g fat; 2g saturated fat; 42g carbohydrate; 0.93g sodium

a curried vegetable and lentil soup

Tamarind concentrate is available in supermarkets and Indian grocery stores – to use, combine 1 part tamarind concentrate with 3 parts water. The soup will keep in the fridge for up to 2 days, or freeze for up to 1 month.

SERVES 3

- 1 onion, chopped
- 4 garlic cloves, chopped
- ½ teaspoon red pepper flakes
- 1 teaspoon freshly ground black pepper
- ½ teaspoon ground cumin
- ½ teaspoon ground coriander
- ½ teaspoon turmeric
- 6 cups vegetable stock, made from 1 bouillon cube and water
- ¾ cup dried red lentils, washed
- 7 ounces butternut squash, cut in chunks
- 2 carrots, sliced
- ½ cup corn
- a heaping ⅓ cup peas (fresh or frozen)
- 4 scallions, sliced
- 1 green chile, seeded and sliced
- 1 tablespoon tamarind/water mixture
- 1 tablespoon fresh cilantro leaves
- a large handful baby spinach leaves
- lime wedges, for squeezing (optional)

1 In a blender or food processor, blend the onion, garlic, red pepper flakes, and spices with a little of the stock until you have an onion puree. Transfer to a large saucepan with the remaining vegetable stock and the lentils.

2 Bring to a boil, then reduce the heat, cover, and simmer for 20 minutes. Add the butternut squash and carrots and cook for another 15 minutes, then add the remaining ingredients and cook for 5 minutes more. Serve with wedges of lime.

PER SERVING: 300 calories; 3g fat; 0.3g saturated fat; 54g carbohydrate; 0.63g sodium

a type of panzanella salad

This quick, Italian-style bread salad will fill you up, and it's quick and easy to prepare.

SERVES 2

- 3 slices soy and linseed bread (see page 49), cut into 3/4-inch cubes
- 2 tablespoons sherry vinegar
- 4 tomatoes, cut into bite-sized chunks
- 4 scallions, roughly chopped
- 1 cucumber, cut in half lengthwise, seeded and cut in 1/2-inch half moon shapes
- 1 x 12-ounce jar whole sweet red peppers in brine, drained and well rinsed, each cut in four
- 1 red chile, seeded and finely chopped
- a handful of arugula, roughly chopped
- 6 basil leaves, shredded
- 3 teaspoons extra virgin olive oil
- freshly ground black pepper

1 Preheat the oven to 400ºF. Place the bread cubes on a baking tray and toast them until golden (10-15 minutes), turning them from time to time. Transfer to a bowl.

2 Sprinkle the bread with the vinegar and set it aside. Combine the remaining ingredients in a bowl and season to taste. Fold in the bread cubes and leave them for 15 minutes before serving to allow the flavors to develop.

PER SERVING: 277 calories; 10g fat; 2g saturated fat; 38g carbohydrate; 0.69g sodium

chunky vegetable soup

We all know by now that we need to eat low GI foods, and this soup contains plenty. It will also freeze well for up to 1 month.

SERVES 6

- cooking spray
- 1 onion, roughly chopped
- 2 garlic cloves, finely chopped
- 2 sage leaves, chopped
- 2 celery stalks, sliced
- 1 leek, sliced
- 2 carrots, sliced
- 6 ounces small new potatoes, cut in half
- 1 x 14 1/2-ounce can chopped tomatoes
- 8 cups vegetable stock
- 1 zucchini, sliced
- 1 cup peas (fresh or frozen)
- 4 ounces green beans, cut in 1 1/4-inch lengths
- 6 ounces Savoy cabbage, finely shredded
- a large handful baby spinach leaves
- 1 x 14-ounce can borlotti beans in water, drained and rinsed
- freshly ground black pepper
- 1 cup finely grated Parmesan cheese, for serving
- 6 slices soy and linseed bread (see page 49), for serving

1 Put a large pot over a medium heat and spray with oil. Add the onion and garlic and cook for 5 minutes until the onion is softening. Add a splash of water as necessary.

2 Add the sage, celery, leek, carrots, and potatoes, and cook for 2 minutes, stirring from time to time. Add the tomatoes and stock and cook for 12-15 minutes, until the potatoes are tender.

3 Add the remaining ingredients and cook for another 5 minutes. Season to taste and serve with the grated Parmesan and bread.

PER SERVING: 294 calories; 8g fat; 2g saturated fat; 39g carbohydrate; 0.74g sodium

classic chicken mood soup

To accompany the soup, offer wedges of lime, thinly sliced red chiles, and sprigs of basil.

- **6 skinless chicken thighs**
- **2½ cups fresh chicken stock**
- **1¼-inch piece of fresh ginger, washed and sliced**
- **2 garlic cloves, bruised**
- **2 tablespoons fish sauce (nam pla)**
- **10 black peppercorns**
- **2 onions, thinly sliced**
- **a good handful of sugarsnap peas, sliced**
- **½ pound broccoli, cut in small pieces**
- **6 scallions, sliced**
- **9 ounces thin rice noodles**
- **3 tablespoons chopped cilantro**

1 Put the chicken in a large pot. Pour in the chicken stock along with 8 cups water and add the ginger, garlic, fish sauce, peppercorns, and onions. Bring just to a boil, then reduce the heat and simmer, covered, for 20 minutes. Remove the chicken and let cool slightly, then cut the meat into shreds or chop it up, and discard the bones. Set the chicken aside until ready to use.

2 Continue to simmer the stock, uncovered, for another 30 minutes or so to reduce it by half. Strain the stock and return to the heat. Skim away any fat that is floating on the surface. Add the sugarsnaps, broccoli, and scallions, and cook for 2 minutes.

3 Meanwhile cover the noodles with boiling water. Soak for 5 minutes, then drain.

4 Return the shredded chicken to the soup. Put the drained noodles into a soup tureen or six individual bowls and top with the chicken soup. Sprinkle with the cilantro.

PER SERVING: 271 calories; 3g fat; 1g saturated fat; 40g carbohydrate; 0.66g sodium

bunho beef with noodles

This is a classic Vietnamese dish. It has a base of fine rice noodles with a light stock and is topped with beef marinated in traditional flavors.

- **1 garlic clove, crushed**
- **1 medium onion, thinly sliced**
- **1 x 2-inch piece of lemongrass, tender inner part only, very finely chopped**
- **1 red chile, seeded and finely chopped**
- **1 teaspoon freshly ground black pepper**
- **1 tablespoon fish sauce (nam pla)**
- **2 teaspoons honey**
- **7 ounces beef tenderloin, thinly sliced**
- **6 ounces fine rice noodles**
- **1¾ cups bean sprouts**
- **4 ounces bok choy, finely shredded**
- **1 cucumber, cut in half lengthwise, seeded and grated**
- **24 mint leaves, thinly sliced**
- **spray oil**
- **1¼ cups fresh beef stock, warmed**
- **1 tablespoon dry-roasted peanuts, chopped**
- **1 teaspoon sesame seeds**

1 In a large bowl, combine the garlic, onion, lemongrass, chile, pepper, fish sauce, and honey, and marinate the beef in this mixture for 30 minutes.

2 Place the rice noodles in a heatproof bowl, cover with boiling water and soak for 5 minutes, then drain. Divide the noodles between 4 individual deep bowls, then add the beansprouts, bok choy, cucumber, and mint.

3 Heat a frying pan or grill pan over a high heat and spray lightly with oil, if necessary. Sear the beef for 30 seconds each side, then add to the bowls. Pour a little stock into each bowl, then sprinkle with the nuts and seeds.

PER SERVING: 295 calories; 7g fat; 2g saturated fat; 44g carbohydrate; 0.47g sodium

smoked trout kedgeree

Race around the supermarket to buy yourself some hot-smoked trout – the remaining ingredients should be in your cupboard.

SERVES 4

- cooking spray
- 1 onion, finely chopped
- 1 tablespoon curry paste
- 1½ cups cooked brown basmati rice
- 7 ounces hot-smoked trout
- 3 tablespoons chopped fresh parsley
- 1 tablespoon chopped chives
- 2 tablespoons no-fat yogurt
- lemon juice, to taste
- freshly ground black pepper, to taste
- 2 hard-boiled eggs, roughly chopped

1 Heat a nonstick frying pan, then spray with oil and fry the onion over a medium heat for 8-10 minutes until softened, but without coloring, adding a splash of water as necessary.
2 Add the curry paste and 1 tablespoon water. Stir to combine, then cook gently for another 3 minutes. Add the rice and cook for 2 minutes more, then flake in the trout and add the herbs and yogurt. Stir to combine and heat through gently to prevent the pieces of trout from falling apart.
3 Season to taste with lemon juice and black pepper, then fold in the hard-boiled eggs.

PER SERVING: 292 calories; 9g fat; 2g saturated fat; 36g carbohydrate; 0.48g sodium

beet, potato, and apple salad

Beets are a great root vegetable, but one that is woefully underused. Watch out for its juices as they can stain clothes and counters.

SERVES 3

- 14 ounces new potatoes, washed
- 1 x 8-ounce package cooked beets in natural juice, cut up small
- 2 dessert apples, cored and thinly sliced
- 1 tablespoon raspberry vinegar (if unavailable, use sherry or another vinegar)
- 1 tablespoon olive oil
- freshly ground black pepper, to taste
- ⅔ cup alfalfa sprouts
- 1 cup cottage cheese
- 1 tablespoon chopped fresh chives

1 Steam or cook the potatoes in boiling water for 15-20 minutes until tender. Drain, and when cool enough to handle, cut into bite-size pieces.
2 Mix the potatoes with the beets and apples in a large serving bowl. Whisk the vinegar, oil, and pepper together, pour it over the salad, and toss to combine.
3 Stir in the alfalfa sprouts, cottage cheese, and chives just before serving.

PER SERVING: 291 calories; 8g fat; 3g saturated fat; 42g carbohydrate; 0.36g sodium

crab cakes with cucumber relish

A delicious light meal that is popular with adults and children, served hot or cold.

SERVES 4

FOR THE CRAB CAKES

- 1 pound cooked crab meat
- 4 scallions, thinly sliced
- 1 teaspoon grated fresh ginger
- 1 red chile, seeded and finely chopped
- ½ red pepper, seeded and finely chopped
- 2 tablespoons finely chopped cilantro
- 1⅓ cups frozen corn kernels, defrosted and well drained
- 2 tablespoons no-fat yogurt
- 1 egg yolk
- ½ cup seeded bread crumbs* see below right
- cooking spray

FOR THE CUCUMBER RELISH

- 1 cucumber, cut in half lengthwise and seeded
- 1 tablespoon sugar
- ¼ cup rice vinegar (or white wine or cider vinegar)
- 1 hot red chile, seeded and finely chopped
- 2 shallots, finely chopped
- ⅓ cup chopped cilantro
- 2½ tablespoons dry-roasted peanuts, chopped
- 2 teaspoons fish sauce (nam pla)

1 Combine all the crab cake ingredients except the bread crumbs and spray oil, and pulse in a food-processor just until the mixture can be pressed together to form 12 cakes. Lightly coat with the bread crumbs, cover, and chill for up to 12 hours.

2 To make the cucumber relish, cut the cucumber in ¼-inch slices. Dissolve the sugar in the vinegar, and toss the cucumber slices in this. Stir in the chile, shallots, and cilantro. Just before serving, sprinkle with the peanuts and add the fish sauce.

3 To cook the crab cakes, spray a light coating of oil in a large nonstick frying pan over a medium heat and add the crab cakes. Do not overcrowd, cook in batches if necessary. Cook for 2–3 minutes on each side until golden and heated through. Serve with the cucumber relish.

* To make the bread crumbs, dry 2–3 slices soy and linseed bread (recipe, page 49) in a preheated oven at 375ºF for about 25 minutes until crisp and brittle. Let cool on a wire rack, then pulse in a food processor until the crumbs are fine but retain some texture.

PER SERVING: 304 calories; 9g fat; 2g saturated fat; 25g carbohydrate; 0.9g sodium

poached baby veg with asparagus and lemon sauce

Every so often I really enjoy a good bowl of vegetables with a very light lemon sauce.
See what you think of this.

SERVES 4

- ■ ⅓ cup farro wheat berries (from spelt) or regular wheat berries, soaked in cold water overnight
- ■ 2½ cups vegetable stock
- ■ 12 baby carrots
- ■ 8 baby turnips
- ■ 12 small new potatoes
- ■ 12 pearl onions
- ■ 16 asparagus spears
- ■ 12 small brussels sprouts
- ■ 10-12 young green beans
- ■ ¾ cup peas (fresh or frozen)
- ■ 4 ounces tiny broccoli florets (about 2 cups)
- ■ 8 cherry tomatoes

FOR THE SAUCE

- ■ 2 egg yolks
- ■ juice of 1-2 lemons
- ■ 2 teaspoons cornstarch
- ■ 2 tablespoons no-fat yogurt
- ■ freshly ground white pepper, to taste

1 Drain and cook the soaked wheat berries in boiling water for about 15 minutes until tender. Drain, and keep warm. Meanwhile, in a large saucepan, bring the vegetable stock to a boil and add the baby carrots, turnips, potatoes, and onions, all left whole. Cook for 12-15 minutes until thoroughly cooked. Remove and set aside to keep warm.

2 Cut the tops off the asparagus spears and reserve, and cook the rest of the stalks in the vegetable stock until tender. Remove and set aside to be used for the sauce.

3 Cook the brussels sprouts in the stock for 3 minutes, then add the beans and cook for another 2 minutes, then add the peas, broccoli, and reserved asparagus spears, and cook for 3 minutes more. Remove all the green vegetables and combine them with the root vegetables in a bowl.

4 Boil the vegetable stock until only 1¼ cups remain. Plunge the cherry tomatoes into the stock and cook for 30 seconds. Remove and add to the other vegetables.

5 To make the sauce, puree the asparagus stalks in a food processor with the egg yolks, the juice of 1 lemon, and the cornstarch, adding a little of the reserved vegetable stock as necessary. Strain the mixture through a fine mesh strainer into a small saucepan. Set over a low heat, then gradually add the hot vegetable stock, whisking constantly until the sauce is lightly thickened but has not boiled. Remove from the heat and whisk in the yogurt. Season to taste with the white pepper and extra lemon juice, as you like.

6 Divide the wheat berries and vegetables between four warm bowls and drizzle with the sauce.

PER SERVING: 289 calories; 7g fat; 1g saturated fat; 44g carbohydrate; 0.23g sodium

Indonesian jumbo shrimp curry

This is one of my favorite curries although it is not Indian by origin – it is much less rich and calorific than a "real" curry would be, but it packs a punch of vibrant flavors. This dish also won the curry challenge on my TV show, *Saturday Cooks*. If you make more than you need, you can always save the leftovers for the next night or put in the freezer.

SERVES 2

FOR THE SHRIMP

- 1 teaspoon lemon juice
- 1 teaspoon turmeric
- ½ teaspoon chili powder
- 7 ounces peeled raw jumbo shrimp, deveined

FOR THE CURRY

- spray canola oil
- 2 medium onions, each cut in 12 wedges
- 4 garlic cloves, sliced
- 1¼-inch piece of fresh ginger, peeled and grated
- 3 green chiles, seeded and sliced
- 1 green pepper, seeded and cut in 1-inch pieces
- 1 teaspoon ground coriander
- 1 teaspoon ground cumin
- 4 tomatoes, cut into chunks
- 1 tablespoon tamarind paste mixed with 3 tablespoons water
- a handful of cilantro leaves, roughly chopped
- sliced scallions, for garnishing
- ½ cup cooked brown basmati rice, for serving

1 Combine the lemon juice, turmeric, and chili powder with 1 tablespoon water, then massage this mixture into the shrimp and let marinate for 20 minutes.

2 Meanwhile, to make the curry base, heat a nonstick wok or frying pan, then spray with oil. Add the onions and cook for 6–8 minutes until the onions are translucent but not brown, adding a splash of water as necessary.

3 Add the garlic, ginger, and chiles and cook for another 2 minutes, then add the green pepper and spices and stir-fry for 3 minutes. Add the tomatoes and tamarind/water mixture, increase the heat, and cook for 3 minutes, adding a little water as necessary.

4 Heat a small nonstick frying pan and spray with oil. Cook the shrimp with their marinade and a splash of water, if necessary, for 2–3 minutes until they turn pink. Fold into the curry sauce and serve at once, sprinkled with cilantro and scallions. Serve with the rice on the side.

PER SERVING: 299 calories; 5g fat; 0.6g saturated fat; 43g carbohydrate; 0.28g sodium

spicy bean baked potato

A quick low-GI chunky dip or filling. Serve with a green salad.

SERVES 4

- 4 x half-pound baking potatoes
- 1 x 15-ounce can red kidney beans in water or cranberry beans in water, drained and rinsed
- ⅔ cup no-fat yogurt
- 2 tomatoes, seeded and chopped
- 1 red chile, seeded and finely chopped
- 1 garlic clove, crushed
- 2 tablespoons chopped cilantro
- 1 teaspoon ground cumin
- 1 teaspoon ground coriander
- ½ small red onion, finely chopped
- juice of ½-1 lime
- freshly ground black pepper, to taste
- green salad, for serving

1 Preheat the oven to 400°F. Scrub the potatoes and prick with a fork. Bake for 50-60 minutes until cooked through, then split them open.
2 Mash half the beans and fold into the yogurt. Add the remaining ingredients along with the whole beans and stir well. Season to taste with pepper and use to fill the split potatoes.

PER SERVING: 298 calories; 2g fat; 0.1g saturated fat; 60g carbohydrate; 0.05g sodium

chicken and salmon miso soup

Surf and Turf (combining seafood and meat) works well with grills, so why not with this main course soup?

SERVES 4

- 2 teaspoons miso paste
- 2 teaspoons oyster sauce
- 2 teaspoons reduced-salt soy sauce
- 1 tablespoon grated ginger
- 1 teaspoon crushed garlic
- finely grated zest and juice of 1 orange
- 4 cups fresh chicken stock
- 7 ounces chicken breast, thinly sliced
- 6 ounces skinless salmon fillet, cut in ½-inch pieces
- 2 heads bok choy, finely shredded
- 4 ounces dried thin wheat noodles, cooked according to package instructions
- 4 scallions, thinly sliced
- freshly ground white pepper, to taste

1 In a large saucepan, combine the miso paste, oyster sauce, soy sauce, ginger, and garlic, and the orange zest and juice. Stir in the stock and bring to a simmer.
2 Add the chicken, salmon, and bok choy. Simmer for 3-4 minutes, then add the cooked noodles and scallions. Season to taste with white pepper.

PER SERVING: 300 calories; 9g fat; 1g saturated fat; 26g carbohydrate; 0.96g sodium

cauliflower rarebit

This is a quick and filling lunch or dinner best served straight from the broiler rather than packed and reheated later.

SERVES 6

- 1¼ pounds cauliflower florets (about 8 cups)
- 3 ounces reduced-fat mature Cheddar cheese, grated (or other strong cheese)
- 1 tablespoon Dijon mustard
- 2 medium eggs, beaten
- 2 teaspoons Worcestershire sauce
- ¼ cup no-fat yogurt
- pinch of grated nutmeg
- freshly ground black pepper, to taste
- 6 slices soy and linseed bread (see page 49), toasted
- ½ pound baby spinach leaves, wilted
- 2 x 15-ounce cans cranberry beans in water, drained, rinsed and warmed
- 12 tomatoes, cut in half and grilled or broiled

1 Preheat the broiler to very hot. Steam or cook the cauliflower in boiling water for about 5 minutes until just tender but retaining some firmness. Drain and keep warm.
2 Meanwhile beat together the cheese, mustard, eggs, Worcestershire sauce, and yogurt with a little nutmeg and black pepper.
3 Place the toast on a baking tray, top with the wilted spinach and warmed beans, then arrange the cauliflower on top. Divide the cheese mixture between the cauliflower toasts, coating the cauliflower evenly. Flash under the broiler until the cheese is bubbling and golden. Serve at once with the grilled tomatoes.

PER SERVING: 330 calories; 9g fat; 2g saturated fat; 39g carbohydrate; 0.74g sodium

avocado dip with pita crisps

This is a great little recipe for a quick snack. The pita crisps can be stored in an airtight container for 4-5 days.

SERVES 3

- 3 pita breads
- a handful of flat-leaf parsley leaves
- a handful of baby spinach leaves
- 1 garlic clove, crushed
- finely grated zest and juice of ½ lemon
- dash of Worcestershire sauce
- dash of Tabasco
- ½ teaspoon ground cumin
- ½ teaspoon ground coriander
- 1 large avocado, peeled and pitted
- ¼ cup no-fat yogurt
- ¼ teaspoon freshly ground black pepper
- 3 tomatoes, cut in wedges, for serving

1 Preheat the oven to 325ºF. Slit the pita in two, then cut each half into 6 triangles and arrange on a baking tray. Bake in the oven for 15-20 minutes until lightly golden and very crispy. Let cool on a wire rack.
2 Meanwhile, bring a pan of water to a boil and plunge in the parsley and spinach. Cook for 2 minutes, then drain and plunge into ice water. Drain, squeeze dry, and roughly chop.
3 Put the spinach mixture in a food processor along with the remaining ingredients except the tomatoes. Pulse until fairly smooth, then check the seasoning. Serve with the tomato wedges and pita crisps.

PER SERVING: 357 calories; 16g fat; 2g saturated fat; 45g carbohydrate; 0.38g sodium

FOR WEIGHT MAINTENANCE
mini low-gi bread and tomato pizza

Prepare the ingredients at home and then whip this up for lunch, so long as you have access to an oven. Instead of using a pizza base or puff pastry, use a low-GI bread – "pizza" in a flash!

SERVES 4

- 1 x 15-ounce can cannellini beans in water, drained and rinsed
- 2 tablespoons black olive paste
- ½ cup pine nuts, toasted
- 3 scallions, finely sliced
- 4 slices soy and linseed bread (or other seeded bread), toasted in the broiler on one side
- 4 tomatoes, sliced
- 1 teaspoon fennel seeds
- ¼ teaspoon chili powder
- 1 tablespoon honey
- 1 tablespoon extra virgin olive oil
- arugula leaves, for serving

1 Preheat the oven to 400ºF. Mash half the beans with the back of a fork. Fold in the remaining beans, the olive paste, pine nuts, and scallions.

2 Spread the untoasted sides of the seeded bread with the bean paste mixture and arrange the sliced tomato on top.

3 Combine the spices with the honey and olive oil and drizzle over the tomatoes. Place the pizza toasts on a baking tray and bake in the oven for 12-15 minutes, until the tomatoes have slightly collapsed. Serve piping hot, with the arugula leaves.

PER SERVING: 353 calories; 19g fat; 2g saturated fat; 35g carbohydrate; 0.4g sodium

FOR WEIGHT MAINTENANCE
mixed grain, seed, and herb salad

We know we should eat them, but how do you make grains and seeds a little more exciting? With the addition of herbs, salad vegetables, and even fruit as here, they can be very flavorsome and enjoyable. This salad will keep in the fridge in an airtight container for up to 48 hours.

SERVES 4

- ⅓ cup wild rice
- ½ cup bulgur
- 3 tablespoons linseeds
- 3½ tablespoons hemp seeds
- 3 tablespoons pumpkin seeds
- 1¾ ounces flat-leaf parsley, roughly chopped
- 3 tablespoons roughly chopped mint
- 3 tablespoons roughly chopped cilantro
- 6 scallions, thinly sliced
- 2 plum tomatoes, chopped
- ½ cup raisins
- ½ cup ready-to-eat dried apricots, chopped
- finely grated zest and juice of 1 lemon
- 1 teaspoon freshly ground black pepper

1 Cook the wild rice according to package instructions. Drain well. Meanwhile, soak the bulgur in 2½ cups boiling water for 15 minutes, then drain and squeeze dry.

2 When cool, combine the rice with the bulgur and seeds, then stir in the herbs, scallions, tomatoes, dried fruit, and lemon zest.

3 Just before serving add the lemon juice and pepper. Toss thoroughly to combine.

PER SERVING: 345 calories; 8g fat; 1g saturated fat; 61g carbohydrate; 0.04g sodium

kippered herring
with apples and horseradish

For breakfast or lunch. A quick dish to put together, but one with lots of taste and texture.

SERVES 4

- 4 Canadian kippers (if unavailable, use hot-smoked salmon)
- 6 tablespoons 0% fat yogurt
- 1 tablespoon lemon juice
- 1 teaspoon grated horseradish
- 1 teaspoon cider vinegar
- 3 dessert apples, cored and finely chopped
- 4 scallions, finely sliced
- freshly ground black pepper, to taste
- 16 crispbreads, for serving

1 Place the herring in a shallow container, cover with boiling water, and leave for 5-7 minutes, then drain thoroughly. Discard the skin, then break the fillets up by shredding the flesh with two forks. Remove as many bones as possible.
2 Put the yogurt in a bowl, then stir in the lemon juice, horseradish, vinegar, apples, and scallions.
3 Fold the fish flakes into this mixture. Season to taste with plenty of black pepper and extra horseradish, if you like. Serve with crispbreads.

PER SERVING: 328 calories; 11g fat; 2g saturated fat; 44g carbohydrate; 0.59g sodium

bean and salad wrap

A versatile quick lunch: eat it warm or cold for something a little different from your average office sandwich.

SERVES 4

- spray canola oil
- 3 scallions, thinly sliced
- 3 garlic cloves, crushed
- 1 red chile, seeded and finely chopped
- 1 teaspoon ground cumin
- 1 teaspoon ground coriander
- 1 cup canned (or fresh) chopped tomatoes
- 1 x 15-ounce can borlotti beans in water, drained and rinsed
- 2 tablespoons chopped cilantro
- 4 flour tortillas, warmed
- 1 medium avocado, peeled and sliced
- 1½ cups shredded iceberg lettuce
- 2 tablespoons no-fat yogurt

1 Heat a nonstick frying pan, spray it with some oil, add the scallions, garlic, and chile and cook for 2 minutes over a medium heat, adding a splash of water if necessary. Add the spices and cook for another minute, then add the tomatoes and beans. Simmer until the liquid has disappeared has reduced to a thick sauce. Stir in the cilantro.
2 Lay the tortillas out on the counter and spread them with some bean mixture, top with avocado and lettuce, and drizzle with the yogurt. Roll the tortillas up, tucking in the ends. Slice in half and eat warm, or for a lunchbox, let them cool, then wrap in waxed paper or plastic wrap.

PER SERVING: 284 calories; 11g fat; 1g saturated fat; 38g carbohydrate; 0.65g sodium

asian chicken and lettuce rolls

This satisfying light lunch is perfect for casual eating. Each person spoons a little of the chicken mixture into the lettuce leaves, rolls them up if they like, and bites into the contrast of the crisp, cool leaves and the warm filling.

SERVES 4

- **14 ounces ground chicken**
- **1 red chile, seeded and finely chopped**
- **2 scallions, finely chopped**
- **1 garlic clove, crushed**
- **1 teaspoon grated ginger**
- **1 teaspoon sesame oil**
- **½ cup chopped water chestnuts or bean sprouts**
- **2 tablespoons chopped cilantro**
- **2 tablespoons chopped cashews**
- **1 carrot, finely chopped**
- **2 tablespoons oyster sauce**
- **2 teaspoons honey**
- **16-20 romaine lettuce leaves**
- **1¾ cups cooked brown basmati rice, for serving**
- **lime wedges, for serving**

1 Mix the chicken with the chile, scallions, garlic, ginger, and sesame oil. Heat a large nonstick frying pan over a medium heat and cook the mixture for about 5 minutes, breaking the meat up with the back of a fork until golden brown.
2 Add the water chestnuts, cilantro, cashews, carrot, oyster sauce, and honey, stir to combine, and continue to heat until the chicken is cooked through.
3 Serve the chicken with the lettuce leaves, the cooked rice, and lime wedges to squeeze over it.

PER SERVING: 343 calories; 7g fat; 1g saturated fat; 45g carbohydrate; 0.49g sodium

more than a mouthful tomato soup

This main course soup has loads of texture and flavor – perfect one-pot dining. Freeze any leftovers in portion-size containers and keep for up to 1 month.

SERVES 4

- **1 large onion, finely chopped**
- **2 garlic cloves, finely chopped**
- **1 x 14½-ounce can chopped tomatoes**
- **1 tablespoon tomato paste**
- **1 dried hot red chile, left whole**
- **2 x 14½-ounce cans chopped tomatoes**
- **2 bay leaves**
- **2 teaspoons ground cumin**
- **1 teaspoon sugar**
- **5 ounces chorizo sausage, skinned and chopped**
- **1 x 15-ounce can cannellini beans in water, drained and rinsed**
- **½ cup brown basmati rice, rinsed**
- **3 tablespoons chopped parsley**
- **freshly ground black pepper, to taste**

1 Put all the ingredients except for the parsley and pepper in a large saucepan. Add 5½ cups litres water, or enough to give you the consistency you prefer, and bring to a simmer. Cover and simmer gently for 30 minutes.
2 Remove the chile and bay leaves, then add the parsley and season to taste. Serve piping hot.

PER SERVING: 326 calories; 11g fat; 4g saturated fat; 42g carbohydrate; 0.43g sodium

main
meals

Here are great
meal ideas for
all occasions –
a sunday roast,
quick chicken
curry, or
veggie pasta.
Make sure you
serve them with
vegetables
and enough
carbohydrates
for your needs.

tomato and wheat bake

SERVES 4

- 1 tablespoon olive oil
- 1 onion, finely chopped
- 2 garlic cloves, finely chopped
- 1 red pepper, seeded and cut into ½-inch squares
- 1 teaspoon each thyme leaves and dried oregano
- 1 x 14½-ounce can chopped tomatoes
- 12 basil leaves, torn
- 1 teaspoon ground allspice and dried chili powder
- 2½ cups vegetable stock
- 1½ cups bulgur
- ¾ cup no-fat yogurt
- 4 medium eggs, beaten
- 2 tablespoons chopped chives
- 3 tomatoes, sliced
- 14 ounces green beans, steamed, for serving

1 Heat the oil in a large saucepan, then add the onion, garlic, and red pepper, and cook gently for 8-10 minutes, adding a splash of water as necessary. Stir in the thyme and oregano and cook for another 5 minutes, adding more water if needed. Stir in the tomatoes and cook for 10 minutes, uncovered, before adding the basil, allspice, and chili.

2 Add the stock to the sauce and bring to a boil. Stir in the bulgur, reduce the heat, and cook for 10-15 minutes, until the bulgur is tender, stirring regularly. The liquid should be all but absorbed.

3 Turn off the heat and let it stand, covered, for 10 minutes. If the mixture is too wet, uncover and cook over a low heat until it becomes thicker. Season to taste with pepper and let it cool.

4 Meanwhile preheat the oven to 350°F, then whisk the yogurt into the eggs and season with pepper and chives. Place the bulgur in a shallow baking dish, top with the sliced tomatoes, then pour the egg mixture over them. Bake in the oven for 30-35 minutes until golden.

PER SERVING: 334 calories; 6g fat; 0.6g saturated fat; 61g carbohydrate; 0.39g sodium

a quick vegetable stir-fry

A vegetarian dish that meat-eaters will also find delicious and that provides a good balance of proteins and carbohydrates.

SERVES 2

- cooking spray
- ½ pound firm tofu, cut into 1-inch pieces
- 2 garlic cloves, crushed
- 1 x 1¼-inch piece of fresh ginger, peeled and grated
- 1 tablespoon hot chili sauce
- ½ pound butternut squash, cut in ½-inch cubes
- 2 tablespoons reduced-salt soy sauce
- 1 teaspoon honey
- 6 ounces button mushrooms, cut in half
- 4 scallions, sliced
- 2 heads bok choy, roughly chopped
- a handful of cilantro leaves
- 1 cup cooked brown basmati rice, for serving

1 Heat a large nonstick frying pan over a high heat, then spray with oil. Cook the tofu pieces in batches until golden on all sides, then remove and set aside.

2 To the same pan, add the garlic, ginger, chili sauce, and butternut squash along with ⅔ cup water and cook until the butternut is starting to soften, about 5 minutes. Add extra water, as necessary.

3 Stir in the soy sauce, honey, and mushrooms, and cook for 3 minutes.

4 Add the scallions and bok choy, and return the tofu to the pan. Cook until the tofu has heated through and the bok choy has wilted, about 2 minutes. Finally fold in the cilantro leaves and serve immediately with the freshly cooked rice.

PER SERVING: 282 calories; 7g fat; 1g saturated fat; 39g carbohydrate; 0.9g sodium

wild mushroom
and barley "risotto"

I like porcini and chanterelles but if you can't find them, use field mushrooms, oyster mushrooms, or shiitake, or a combination. Serve with a green salad.

SERVES 4

- 1 tablespoon olive oil
- 1 onion, finely chopped
- 2 garlic cloves, finely chopped
- 1 teaspoon soft thyme leaves
- 1 bay leaf
- 12 ounces assorted mushrooms, wiped and sliced
- 1⅓ cups barley, rinsed
- ⅓ cup red wine
- 3-4 cups vegetable stock, heated
- 1½ cups frozen peas, defrosted
- 2 large handfuls baby spinach leaves
- 3 tablespoons chopped parsley
- freshly ground black pepper, to taste

1 Heat the oil in a large pot over a medium heat. Add the onion, garlic, thyme, and bay leaf, and cook gently, stirring occasionally for 8-10 minutes. Add a splash of water as necessary.

2 Stir in the mushrooms and cook for 4-5 minutes, again adding a splash of water as necessary. Add the barley and stir. Pour in the wine and let it boil until evaporated.

3 Add a ladleful of stock and simmer, uncovered, until it has been absorbed. Repeat the process until 3 cups of stock have been absorbed – about 30 minutes – and the barley is tender.

4 Stir in the peas, spinach, and parsley, and simmer for 5 minutes, adding the extra stock if you want a soft risotto consistency. Season to taste with pepper.

PER SERVING: 353 calories; 6g fat; 1g saturated fat; 64g carbohydrate; 0.44g sodium

FOR WEIGHT MAINTENANCE

penne with
artichokes and
arugula pesto

A store-cupboard pasta dish - all you need to buy is some feta and the greens.

SERVES 4

- 11 ounces dried penne, or other pasta shape
- a large handful arugula leaves
- a small handful baby spinach leaves
- 1 tablespoon slivered almonds, toasted
- 2 garlic cloves, chopped
- ½ teaspoon dried red pepper flakes
- finely grated zest and juice of 1 lemon
- 1 tablespoon capers, rinsed and drained
- 2 tablespoons finely grated Parmesan cheese
- 1 x 10-ounce jar wood-roasted artichokes, drained, well rinsed and each one cut in half
- freshly ground black pepper
- ½ cup crumbled feta cheese

1 Cook the pasta according to the package instructions.

2 Meanwhile, in a food processor, pulse together half the arugula, all the spinach, almonds, garlic, red pepper flakes, lemon zest and juice, capers, and Parmesan, then transfer to a bowl.

3 Drain the pasta, retaining ⅓ cup cooking water. Add the water to the pesto, then add the pesto and artichokes to the pasta, toss to combine, and return to a very gentle heat to warm it through.

4 Stir in the reserved arugula leaves and season with pepper. Transfer to warm bowls and top with the crumbled feta. Serve immediately.

PER SERVING: 444 calories; 18g fat; 4g saturated fat; 60g carbohydrate; 0.7g sodium

spaghetti with zucchini, ricotta, basil, and lemon

Keep the zucchini al dente, and, if you can find some, try using spelt spaghetti for a change.

SERVES 4

- 11 ounces dried spaghetti
- 1 tablespoon olive oil
- 2 garlic cloves, finely chopped
- 2 zucchini, thinly sliced
- finely grated zest and juice of 1 lemon
- 2 ounces ricotta cheese, crumbled
- 1 tablespoon grated Parmesan cheese
- 2 tomatoes, finely chopped
- 8 basil leaves, torn into pieces
- 1 tablespoon pine nuts, toasted
- freshly ground black pepper, to taste

1 Cook the pasta in boiling water for 1 minute less than the recommended time on the package. Drain, reserving a little of the cooking water.
2 Meanwhile, heat the olive oil in a large frying pan or wok and fry the garlic and zucchini over a medium heat, turning regularly, for about 3 minutes until just starting to color.

3 Add the pasta to the zucchini together with 3-4 tablespoons cooking water. Stir in the lemon zest and juice, both cheeses, the tomatoes, basil, and toasted pine nuts, and toss to combine. Season with pepper and serve immediately.

PER SERVING: 349 calories; 8g fat; 2g saturated fat; 59g carbohydrate; 0.04g sodium

hot shrimp, cold salad

The taste sensations in this salad work well together, as does the contrast between hot and cold.

SERVES 2

FOR THE SHRIMP

- 1 garlic clove, crushed
- ³/₄-inch piece of fresh ginger, peeled and grated
- 2 tablespoons chopped cilantro
- 1 tablespoon chopped mint
- ¼ teaspoon dried red pepper flakes
- 2 teaspoons honey
- ½ pound shelled raw shrimp, ideally with tails intact, rinsed
- ½ cup cooked brown basmati rice

FOR THE SALAD

- ½ cucumber, sliced lengthwise, seeded and cut in ¼-inch-thick half moons
- 1 small red onion, cut in half and thinly sliced
- 16 cherry tomatoes, cut in half
- 1 tablespoon sunflower seeds
- 1 red chile, seeded and thinly sliced
- 3 tablespoons cilantro leaves
- 1 tablespoon chopped mint leaves
- 1 tablespoon basil leaves, torn into pieces
- 1 teaspoon fish sauce (nam pla)
- juice of 1 lime
- ½ teaspoon sugar

1 For the shrimp, pulse together in a mini food processor the garlic, ginger, cilantro, mint, red pepper flakes, and honey to form a smooth paste. Alternatively, very finely chop the garlic, ginger, and herbs, then stir in the red pepper flakes and honey. Toss the shrimp in this paste, cover, and let marinate in the fridge for at least 30 minutes or up to 12 hours.

2 Meanwhile prepare the salad. In a large bowl, combine the cucumber, onion, tomatoes, sunflower seeds, chile, and herbs, and set aside. Mix together the fish sauce, lime juice, and sugar, and stir until the sugar has dissolved. Set aside.

3 Start the water boiling in a steamer. Place the shrimp in a dish in the steamer, cover, and cook over a high heat for 4 minutes. You will most probably have to do this in two batches.

4 Just before serving, pour the dressing over the salad and toss to combine. Divide between two plates and serve with the hot shrimp. Serve the rice separately.

PER SERVING: 296 calories; 5g fat; 0.7g saturated fat; 37g carbohydrate; 0.51g sodium

spiced cod on a bed of chorizo-infused beans

You may need extra carbs with this meal.

SERVES 4

- 2 ounces chorizo, skinned and cut into cubes
- 1 onion, chopped
- 1 garlic clove, crushed
- 1 teaspoon oregano leaves, roughly chopped
- 9 ounces shelled fresh or frozen baby edamame beans (or 4 ounces frozen fava or lima beans)
- 18 ounces new potatoes, cut into 1/4-inch slices
- 1/2 teaspoon each ground cumin and coriander
- 1 teaspoon paprika
- 1/2 teaspoon turmeric
- 2 teaspoons honey
- lemon juice, to taste
- 4 x 4-ounce cod fillets with skin
- spray olive oil

1 Put the chorizo in a hot nonstick pan and cook over a medium heat until it releases its red oils. Add the onion, garlic, and oregano leaves, and cook for 5-7 minutes until the onion has softened, adding a splash of water, as necessary.
2 Add the beans and potatoes with 1 cup water. Cover with a circle of wet baking paper and a lid and cook over a very low heat for 30-40 minutes. Do not let it dry out, top up with water as needed.
3 Meanwhile preheat the oven to 425°F. Combine the spices with the honey and enough lemon juice to make a thin paste. Use to coat the flesh side of the cod.
4 Spray a nonstick ovenproof frying pan with olive oil. Over a high heat, cook the cod, skin side down, for 5 minutes, then place in the oven for 10 minutes until golden and very lightly caramelized.
5 Divide the bean mixture between four warm plates, then top with the cod.

PER SERVING: 290 calories; 5g fat; 1g saturated fat; 31g carbohydrate; 0.16g sodium

stovetop vegetable stew

Oats aren't just for breakfast, here they help thicken this vegetarian stew.

SERVES 4

- 1 tablespoon olive oil
- 1 onion, finely chopped
- 2 large leeks (washed), cut in 3/4-inch rings
- 3 garlic cloves, crushed
- 1 fennel bulb, chopped
- 3/4 cup rolled oats
- 5 cups vegetable stock
- 1 medium potato, cut in 3/4-inch cubes
- 1 x 14 1/2-ounce can chopped tomatoes
- 2 large zucchini, cut in 3/4-inch pieces
- 1/2 butternut squash, peeled and cut in 3/4-inch cubes
- 1/2 savoy cabbage, roughly chopped
- a few sprigs of thyme
- 2 bay leaves
- 3 large handfuls spinach leaves, washed and large stalks removed
- 1/2 teaspoon grated nutmeg
- pinch of ground allspice
- freshly ground black pepper, to taste

1 Heat the olive oil in a heavy pot on the stove and add the onion, leeks, garlic, and fennel, and cook gently for 8-10 minutes until the vegetables have softened. Add a splash of water, as necessary.
2 Stir in the oats and cook over a slightly higher heat until the oats have turned lightly golden, stirring regularly. Remove from the heat.
3 Meanwhile heat the stock to boiling in a large pot, then add the potato and the tomatoes and simmer for 10 minutes. Add the zucchini, squash, and cabbage, along with the thyme and bay leaves. Simmer for another 10 minutes.
4 Fold in the spinach, spices, and oat mixture. Cook for 10 minutes until thick. Season to taste.

PER SERVING: 332 calories; 9g fat; 1g saturated fat; 47g carbohydrate; 0.76g sodium

steak with beans and greens

SERVES 4

- 1 cup dried small pasta shapes
- 1 teaspoon olive oil
- 1 onion, thinly sliced
- large pinch of red pepper flakes
- 1 garlic clove, crushed
- 1 x 15-ounce can white beans (such as navy beans or cannellini) in water, drained and rinsed
- 2 large handfuls baby spinach leaves
- 4 tablespoons chopped parsley
- 12 ounces lean rump, sirloin or tenderloin steak, cut thickly
- freshly ground black pepper, to taste

FOR THE VINAIGRETTE

- finely grated zest and juice of 1 unwaxed lemon
- 1 tablespoon Dijon mustard
- 1 shallot, finely chopped
- 2 tablespoons baby capers, rinsed
- 1 teaspoon chopped anchovies or anchovy paste
- $\frac{1}{4}$ teaspoon freshly ground black pepper

1 First make the vinaigrette by combining all the ingredients with 2 tablespoons ice water and set aside.

2 Cook the pasta. Heat the olive oil in a large saucepan then add the onion, red pepper flakes, and garlic, and cook over a medium heat for 6-8 minutes until softened but not browned. Add a splash of water, as necessary.

3 Stir in the beans and cook until warm, then fold in the spinach and parsley and cook until wilted. Stir in the cooked pasta and half the vinaigrette.

4 Meanwhile season the steak with pepper and cook on a preheated grill pan until charred on both sides and cooked to your liking. Let the meat rest for 5 minutes, then slice thinly.

5 Divide the beans, then top with steak and drizzle with the remaining vinaigrette and any meat juices.

PER SERVING: 304 calories; 6g fat; 2g saturated fat; 35g carbohydrate; 0.43g sodium

asian chicken salad

A crunchy Asian salad that is light to eat and easy to prepare.

SERVES 2

- 1 medium chicken breast, cooked and finely shredded
- 1 large shallot, thinly sliced
- 1$\frac{3}{4}$ cups bean sprouts, rinsed
- 2$\frac{1}{2}$ cups finely shredded Chinese cabbage
- 1 large carrot, very thinly sliced
- 1 cucumber, cut in half lengthwise, seeded and cut in $\frac{1}{4}$-inch slices
- $\frac{3}{4}$ cup cherry tomatoes, cut in half
- 8 radishes, sliced
- 2 tablespoons cilantro leaves
- 1 tablespoon shredded mint leaves
- 2 tablespoons unsalted dry-roasted peanuts, chopped
- 2 ounces rice vermicelli, prepared according to package instructions and well drained

FOR THE DRESSING

- $\frac{1}{4}$ cup lime juice
- 1 tablespoon fish sauce (nam pla)
- 2 bird's-eye chiles (Thai chiles), seeded and finely chopped
- 2 garlic cloves, crushed
- 2 teaspoons honey

1 Combine all the dressing ingredients in a small bowl or measuring cup and let sit for 30 minutes to allow the flavors to develop.

2 Combine all the salad ingredients apart from the noodles in a large bowl.

3 Just before serving, toss the dressing through the salad until well mixed.

4 Spoon the noodles into 2 large bowls and top with the salad.

PER SERVING: 337 calories; 9g fat; 2g saturated fat; 39g carbohydrate; 0.66g sodium

white bean and lamb stew

A great winter-warming dish, easy to prepare and very satisfying. Freeze any leftovers.

- spray olive oil
- 11 ounces very lean lamb (from the leg or neck fillet), cut into small pieces
- 1 onion, roughly chopped
- 2 celery stalks, cut into ¾-inch chunks
- 2 carrots, peeled and cut into ¾-inch chunks
- 2 garlic cloves, sliced
- 2 sprigs of rosemary
- 1 tablespoon Worcestershire sauce
- 1 x 14½-ounce can chopped tomatoes
- 2 bay leaves
- 2 x 15-ounce cans black-eyed peas in water, drained and rinsed
- 11 ounces savoy cabbage, roughly chopped
- freshly ground black pepper, to taste

1 Preheat the oven to 350°F.

2 Heat a heavy flameproof and ovenproof pot over a high heat, then spray lightly with oil and fry the lamb in batches until browned all over. Set aside.

3 To the same pot, add the onion, celery, carrots, garlic, and rosemary, and cook, adding a splash of water, until the vegetables have started to soften – 8-10 minutes.

4 Return the lamb to the pot and add the Worcestershire sauce, tomatoes, and bay leaves. Stir to combine, then add 1¼ cups water. Cover and cook in the oven for 45 minutes, then stir in the beans and cabbage, adding extra water as necessary. Return to the oven for another 15 minutes. Season with pepper to taste.

PER SERVING: 316 calories; 8g fat; 2g saturated fat; 35g carbohydrate; 0.21g sodium

an andalucian pork stew

If you're not a fan of blood sausage, use an extra 4 ounces of pork tenderloin instead. If you make more than you need, you can freeze half.

- spray olive oil
- 7 ounces pork tenderloin, cut into 1-inch pieces
- 1 onion, roughly chopped
- 2 celery stalks, chopped
- 2 carrots, thinly sliced
- 3 garlic cloves, finely chopped
- 5 ounces green beans, topped and tailed
- 2 cups chicken stock
- 1 x 15-ounce can chickpeas in water, drained and rinsed
- 1 x 15-ounce can cannellini beans in water, drained and rinsed
- 4 ounces blood sausage, cut up small
- 2 red peppers, charred and peeled, seeded and cut into strips, can buy these in a jar, well rinsed
- freshly ground black pepper, to taste

1 Heat a large nonstick pan over a high heat and spray with oil. Add the pork to the pan and brown it all over. Remove and set aside. Add the onion, celery, and carrots to the pan and cook gently, adding a splash of water as necessary until they start to soften. Stir in the garlic, green beans, and the stock, and simmer for 8-10 minutes.

2 Return the browned meat to the pan. Add the chickpeas and cannellini beans and bring to a simmer. Cover and cook over a low heat for 2-3 minutes.

3 Meanwhile dry-fry the blood sausage in a small nonstick frying pan. Add the blood sausage and the pimiento or peppers to the stew and cook for another 5 minutes. Season with pepper to taste.

PER SERVING: 350 calories; 11g fat; 1g saturated fat; 38g carbohydrate; 0.8g sodium

paprika tuna with green and white pea mash

Simple, yet tasty and very quick to make.

SERVES 4

- ½ teaspoon olive oil
- 1 teaspoon sweet paprika
- 1 teaspoon coarsely ground black pepper
- 4 thick tuna fillets, about 4 ounces each
- cooking spray
- 4 ounces watercress, well washed and with large stalks removed
- lemon juice or red wine vinegar, for sprinkling
- 18 ounces new potatoes, boiled in their skins, for serving

FOR THE MASH

- ⅔ cup chicken stock
- 2 cups frozen peas
- 2 x 15-ounce cans chickpeas in water, drained and rinsed
- squeeze of lemon juice

1 Preheat the oven to 425ºF.

2 Mix the olive oil with the paprika and pepper and coat the tuna with it. Lightly spray a baking tray with oil and place the tuna on this. Bake for 4-5 minutes for medium rare or 7-8 minutes for more well cooked.

3 Meanwhile make the mash. Bring the stock to a boil in a saucepan. Add the frozen peas and boil for 2 minutes. Stir in the chickpeas and cook until they are heated through and most of the stock has evaporated. Remove from the heat, roughly mash with a potato masher, and season to taste with lemon juice and pepper.

4 Sprinkle the tuna with the lemon juice or red wine vinegar and serve on a bed of pea mash with the watercress and boiled potatoes on the side.

PER SERVING: 399 calories; 8g fat; 1g saturated fat; 47g carbohydrate; 0.21g sodium

---

herby mackerel

SERVES 4

- 4 small mackerel (about 6½ ounces each)
- 1 slice soy and linseed bread (see page 49)
- 1 tablespoon each chopped parsley and cilantro
- finely grated zest of 1 lemon and 1 orange
- ½ teaspoon each ground cumin and ground coriander
- pinch of chili flakes
- ½ teaspoon olive oil
- 3½ fluid ounces fish or chicken stock
- 1¼ pounds new potatoes, cooked

FOR THE TOMATO SALAD

- 6-8 medium-sized tomatoes, sliced
- ½ medium red onion, very thinly sliced
- 1 tablespoon each chopped parsley and cilantro
- 2 teaspoons orange or lemon juice
- freshly ground black pepper

1 Preheat the oven to 400ºF.

2 Remove the heads from the mackerel then split along the belly and remove the guts. Wash thoroughly and pat dry with a paper towel. Open out each fish so that it lies skin-side up and press firmly along the length to loosen the backbone. Carefully lift the bone from the flesh then cut off at the tail end leaving the tail intact. Rinse and dry.

3 In a food-processor, pulse the bread with the herbs, zests, spices, chili flakes, and olive oil until it makes fine crumbs.

4 Arrange the mackerel flesh-side up in a large baking dish and sprinkle with the breadcrumbs. Pour the stock around the mackerel but not over.

5 Cook in the oven for 8-10 minutes until the fish is opaque.

6 Meanwhile, combine all the salad ingredients. Serve the mackerel with any juices from the baking dish and the salad and potatoes.

PER SERVING: 430 calories; 22g fat; 4g saturated fat; 33g carbohydrate; 0.23g sodium

herb and nut-crusted sole

Dover or lemon, the choice is yours, but I think lemon sole represents excellent value and this topping gives the fish another dimension.

SERVES 4

- 1 tablespoon chopped chives
- 2 tablespoons chopped flat-leaf parsley
- 1 teaspoon rosemary leaves
- 1 slice day-old seeded bread, crusts removed
- juice of ½ lemon
- 2 tablespoons dry-toasted hazelnuts or slivered almonds, chopped
- 2 teaspoons flour, for dusting
- paprika, to taste
- freshly ground black pepper, to taste
- 4 x 4-ounce fillets of lemon or Dover sole, skin on
- 1 egg, beaten
- spray olive oil
- lemon wedges, for serving

FOR THE VEGETABLES

- 12 ounces new potatoes, cut in wedges and cooked
- spray olive oil
- ½ teaspoon finely chopped rosemary leaves
- paprika, to taste
- freshly ground black pepper, to taste
- 1¾ cups baby fava beans or limas, fresh or frozen, and skinned if you prefer
- 1 cup peas, fresh or frozen

1 Put the chives, parsley, rosemary, bread, and lemon juice in a food processor and blend to fine green crumbs. Stir in the nuts and set aside.

2 For the vegetables, preheat the oven to 400°F. Place the potatoes in a nonstick roasting pan and spray them with a light coating of olive oil. Season with rosemary, paprika and ground black pepper. Cook for about 20 minutes, turning from time to time, until lightly crisp. Meanwhile, boil the fava (or lima) beans and peas – 3 minutes for frozen or up to 10 minutes for fresh. Drain and toss with the potatoes and keep warm.

3 For the fish: season the flour with paprika and black pepper and dust the flesh side of the fish with the flour. Put the beaten egg in a shallow plate. Put the nut crumb mixture in another. Dip the floured flesh side of each fillet first in the egg, and then the crumbs, pressing gently to ensure an even coating.

4 Heat a large ovenproof frying pan, ideally nonstick, and spray with a light mist of olive oil. Place the fish in the pan, skin-side down, and cook for 3 minutes. Turn them and transfer to the preheated oven, and cook for 6 minutes.

5 Divide the vegetables between four warm plates, then top with the breaded sole. Serve with lemon wedges for squeezing.

PER SERVING: 297 calories; 8g fat; 2g saturated fat; 29g carbohydrate; 0.19g sodium

trout in a pea and artichoke stew

FOR WEIGHT MAINTENANCE

You can now buy fillets from large trout that look very similar to salmon, but are cheaper.

SERVES 4

- 1 x 9-ounce jar wood-roasted artichokes, drained and rinsed
- finely grated zest and juice of 1 lemon
- 2 cups vegetable stock
- 1 tablespoon chopped thyme
- 1 pound, 10 ounces new potatoes, chopped
- 14 ounces frozen peas
- 3¼ cups baby cups trout fillet, cut in ¾-inch cubes
- 4 tablespoons chopped parsley
- freshly ground black pepper, to taste

1 Put the artichokes, lemon zest and juice, stock, thyme, and potatoes in a wide, shallow, heavy pot, and cook, covered, over a medium heat for about 25 minutes until the potatoes are tender. Add a little water, as necessary.

2 Add the peas and trout and cook gently for another 5-7 minutes until the fish is just opaque. Sprinkle with parsley and season to taste with pepper. Serve in warm bowls.

PER SERVING: 445 calories; 18g fat; 3g saturated fat; 42g carbohydrate; 0.67g sodium

spiced mussels (or clams) with tomatoes

Scrub the mussel shells well to remove any grit and pull off the "beards." Rinse thoroughly, discarding any with broken shells or that do not close when tapped hard on a counter.

SERVES 2

- 1 teaspoon olive oil
- 1 onion, finely chopped
- 2 garlic cloves, crushed
- ½ teaspoon red pepper flakes
- 1 teaspoon ground cumin
- 1 teaspoon ground coriander
- ½ teaspoon turmeric
- ⅓ cup dry white wine
- 1 x 14½-ounce can chopped tomatoes
- 2¼ pounds mussels (or clams), thoroughly cleaned
- 2 tablespoons chopped parsley
- finely grated zest of 1 lemon
- 2 slices oat, soy and linseed bread (see page 49), for serving

1 Heat the olive oil in a deep pot, add the onion, and cook over a medium heat for 6 minutes until translucent. Add half the garlic, all the red pepper flakes and spices, and cook for another 2 minutes, stirring regularly. Add the white wine and heat through for 3-4 minutes, then add the tomatoes and bring to a boil.

2 Add the mussels or clams and cook, covered with a lid, over a high heat for 4-6 minutes, shaking the pot from time to time until the shells open.

3 Transfer the mussels to four warm bowls, discarding any that have not opened, then stir the remaining garlic, the parsley, and lemon zest into the sauce. Cook for 1 minute, then pour it over the mussels. Serve with the seeded bread.

PER SERVING: 335 calories; 8g fat; 1g saturated fat; 36g carbohydrate; 0.72g sodium

baked sardines with tomato

SERVES 4

- 8 medium sardines, filleted
  (14 ounces filleted weight. If unavailable, use young herring or similar small fish)
- 4 small tomatoes
- freshly ground black pepper
- finely grated zest of ½ lemon
- 2½ ounces lowfat mozzarella, drained and diced
- 1 teaspoon fresh thyme leaves
- 3½ ounces baby spinach leaves, for serving

FOR THE SWEET POTATOES

- 2 sweet potatoes, peeled and cut into chunks
- juice of ½ lemon
- 1 teaspoon fresh thyme leaves
- ½ teaspoon freshly ground black pepper

1 Preheat the oven to 425ºF. Toss the sweet potatoes with the flavoring ingredients and transfer to a non-stick roasting pan. Bake for 40 minutes, turning occasionally, until tender.

2 Prepare the sardines: discard the heads and guts and wash thoroughly, removing any black membrane from inside the gut cavity. Turn the fish skin-side up and press along the backbone from head to tail to loosen. Remove the back bone. Rinse thoroughly and dry on paper towels.

3 Dice the tomatoes and set them in a sieve over a small bowl to collect all the juices. Arrange the sardines flesh-side up on a non-stick baking tray and season with pepper.

4 Mix the well-drained tomatoes with the lemon zest, diced mozzarella, and thyme and pile onto the fish fillets. Cook in the oven for 10 minutes.

5 Add the reserved tomato juice to the sweet potatoes and return to the oven while the fish cooks. Serve the sardines and sweet potatoes at once with a handful of fresh spinach leaves.

PER SERVING: 339 calories; 12g fat; 3g saturated fat; 34g carbohydrate; 0.23g sodium

FOR WEIGHT MAINTENANCE tuna, pink grapefruit, and avocado salad

A lovely refreshing salad that is light yet full of healthy goodness.

SERVES 2

- 1 pink grapefruit
- 1 small avocado, peeled, pitted and chopped
- 1 x 15-ounce can cannellini beans (or other white beans) in water, drained and rinsed
- 7 ounces canned tuna in spring water, drained and flaked
- a large handful baby spinach leaves
- 2 slices oat, soy, and linseed bread (see page 49), for serving

FOR THE DRESSING

- 1 tablespoon raspberry vinegar (or other vinegar)
- ½ medium red onion, finely chopped
- 1 teaspoon honey
- 2 teaspoons fish sauce (nam pla)
- 1 tablespoon chopped cilantro
- 1 teaspoon chopped mint

1 Using a small serrated knife, peel the grapefruit, discarding all the white pith. Cut between the membranes of the grapefruit to extract the segments. Do this over a bowl to catch the juices, then squeeze the grapefruit trimmings after you have taken all the segments out. You should end up with about 4 tablespoons juice. Reserve the juice and put the segments in a bowl.

2 Add the avocado, beans, and tuna to the grapefruit and toss to combine.

3 Add the dressing ingredients to the grapefruit juice and whisk to combine, then pour it over the grapefruit salad. Add the spinach leaves and toss lightly. Serve at once with the bread.

PER SERVING: 441 calories; 14g fat; 2g saturated fat; 49g carbohydrate; 0.6g sodium

poached salmon and tahini sauce
with eggplant salad

Poaching keeps the salmon wonderfully moist. A microwave, if you have one, is a good way to cook the eggplant – prick it and cook at high heat for 5 minutes, then chop once it's cooled slightly.

SERVES 4

- 2 onions, sliced
- 4 x 4-ounce salmon fillets
- ½ cup bulgur, cooked according to package instructions

FOR THE TAHINI SAUCE

- ⅔ cup no-fat yogurt
- 1 tablespoon tahini
- 1 garlic clove, crushed
- lemon juice, to taste
- ½ teaspoon freshly ground black pepper

FOR THE EGGPLANT SALAD

- ¼ cup walnut pieces
- 1 tablespoon sesame seeds
- 1 medium eggplant, cut into ¾-inch chunks
- 1 tomato, finely chopped
- 1 small red onion, finely chopped
- a small handful of flat-leaf parsley leaves, finely shredded
- a small handful of cilantro leaves, finely shredded
- a small handful of fenugreek leaves (optional)
- 1 garlic clove, crushed
- ½ teaspoon sumac (optional)
- juice of 1 lemon
- freshly ground black pepper, to taste

1 For the eggplant salad, preheat the oven to 350ºF. Spread the walnuts and sesame seeds onto a baking tray and cook for 8-10 minutes, shaking them around from time to time so they color evenly. Once cool, roughly chop.

2 Steam the eggplant cubes for 10 minutes or until tender. Tip into a colander and leave to cool then squeeze it gently to extract some of its water. Just before serving, combine with the rest of the salad ingredients.

3 For the salmon, pour 3 cups water into a wide, shallow saucepan and add the sliced onions. Bring to a simmer, then add the salmon and poach, covered, for 10 minutes. Carefully lift the salmon out of its poaching liquor and transfer to paper towels to drain. Let cool slightly, then peel off the skin and, if you like, gently scrape away the dark flesh on the underside.

4 Meanwhile, prepare the tahini sauce by whisking all the ingredients together until smooth.

5 Serve the salmon at room temperature with the bulgur, salad, and tahini sauce.

PER SERVING: 446 calories; 21g fat; 4g saturated fat; 30g carbohydrate; 0.09g sodium

quick chicken curry

This is a delicious light curry, perfect for a week-night supper. If you make more than you need, you could freeze and reheat the curry – but don't freeze the rice.

SERVES 4

- 1 tablespoon canola oil
- 1 onion, sliced
- 1 teaspoon finely chopped garlic
- 1 teaspoon grated ginger
- 2 green chiles, seeded and finely chopped
- 2 large zucchini, cut in half lengthwise, then sliced
- 1 teaspoon turmeric
- 3 tomatoes, each cut into 8 pieces
- 1$\frac{1}{4}$ cups frozen peas
- 14 ounces cooked chicken, cut in bite-size pieces
- 2 large handfuls baby spinach leaves
- 4 tablespoons chopped cilantro
- 1 tablespoon garam masala
- 1$\frac{1}{3}$ cups cooked brown basmati rice

1 Heat the oil in a large, wide, nonstick pot or wok. Add the onion and cook, covered, over a medium heat until softened but not browned, 8-10 minutes. Stir in the garlic, ginger, and chiles, and cook for another minute.

2 Add the zucchini and turmeric, pour in $\frac{1}{4}$ cup water, then cover and cook over a gentle heat for 10-12 minutes until the zucchini have softened. Stir from time to time.

3 Add the tomatoes and stir to combine. Cover and cook for 4-5 minutes until the tomatoes have softened.

4 Stir in the peas, chicken, spinach, cilantro, and garam masala with another $\frac{1}{4}$-$\frac{1}{3}$ cup water. Cook for about 5 minutes until the chicken is heated through and the spinach has wilted. Serve with the freshly cooked basmati rice.

PER SERVING: 427 calories; 13g fat; 3g saturated fat; 44g carbohydrate; 0.13g sodium

broiled chicken with stir-fried spinach and lentils

A good, healthy way to end the day, this isn't just any old broiled chicken,
but one packed with flavor.

SERVES 4

- ½ teaspoon ground cumin
- ½ teaspoon ground coriander
- ½ teaspoon freshly ground black pepper
- 4 x 4-ounce chicken breast fillets, skinless
- spray olive oil

FOR THE MANGO YOGURT

- 1 medium mango cut in ½-inch cubes
- 1 red chile, seeded and finely chopped
- ½ tablespoon chopped mint
- 1 tablespoon mango chutney
- 1 teaspoon curry paste
- ⅔ cup no-fat yogurt

FOR THE SPINACH

- 1 cup red lentils
- 1 tablespoon canola oil
- 3 garlic cloves, bruised
- 1 dried chile
- 18 ounces baby spinach leaves, washed
- 1 tablespoon reduced-salt soy sauce
- freshly ground black pepper, to taste
- 2½ tablespoons dry-roasted peanuts, chopped

1 First make the mango yogurt: combine the mango, chile, and mint, and set aside. Mix the chutney and curry paste together, then fold in the yogurt. Combine the yogurt with the mango and set aside for at least 30 minutes for the flavors to infuse.

2 When ready to cook the chicken, preheat the broiler to high. Combine the three spices and dust the chicken breasts with the mixture. Spray the chicken lightly with oil and cook under the preheated broiler for 7-8 minutes on each side, turning once. Set aside to keep warm.

3 Meanwhile, cook the lentils in boiling water for 7-8 minutes until tender yet still with a little "bite." Drain thoroughly. Heat a large wok until very hot then add the oil, garlic, and chile, and cook until the garlic is deep golden and the chile has turned dark brown. Discard the garlic and chile from the oil, add the spinach a little at a time over a high heat until wilted. Stir in the lentils, then add the soy sauce and pepper to taste.

4 Pile the spinach mixture onto four warm plates. Slice the chicken (it looks like more that way!) and arrange it over the spinach, sprinkle with the peanuts, and serve with the mango yogurt.

PER SERVING: 443 calories; 10g fat; 2g saturated fat; 40g carbohydrate; 0.53g sodium

sausages with white beans and roasted peppers

A great way of getting more from a few sausages. Be sure to choose good-quality sausages with a high meat content.

SERVES 2

- 7 ounces extra lean pork sausages (about 4 thin sausages or 2 Italian sausages), cut in 1-inch chunks
- cooking spray
- 4 garlic cloves, finely chopped
- 1 onion, roughly chopped
- 1 x 12-ounce jar whole sweet red peppers in brine, drained, rinsed and roughly chopped
- 1 x 15-ounce can cannellini beans in water, drained and rinsed
- 5 ounces baby spinach leaves
- 4 tablespoons chopped flat-leaf parsley
- finely grated zest and juice of ½ lemon
- freshly ground black pepper, to taste

1 Preheat the broiler to high and cook the sausage pieces until brown all over, then remove and set aside.

2 Heat a large nonstick pan over a medium heat and spray with oil. Add half the garlic and all the onion to the pan and cook gently, adding a splash of water as necessary, until the onion is translucent, about 8 minutes.

3 Add the peppers, beans, and ¼ cup water and cook for 5 minutes. Add the sausages and spinach and cook for another 5 minutes.

4 Meanwhile, in a mini food processor or mortar and pestle, blend together the remaining garlic, the parsley, and lemon zest and juice. Add this to the pan and stir well. Season with pepper to taste and serve immediately.

PER SERVING: 393 calories; 9g fat; 2g saturated fat; 47g carbohydrate; 0.86g sodium

rice noodles with chicken, shrimp, and squid

This is a really quick and easy stir-fry that also contains lots of green veg.

SERVES 4

- 9 ounces rice noodles
- spray canola oil
- 4 garlic cloves, crushed
- 2 red chiles, seeded and finely chopped
- 1 skinless chicken breast fillet, finely shredded
- 1 medium egg, beaten
- 1 tablespoon reduced-salt soy sauce
- 1 tablespoon oyster sauce
- 4 ounces sugarsnap peas, coarsely shredded
- 4 ounces Savoy cabbage, finely shredded
- 1 cup bean sprouts
- 6 ounces prepared squid, cut in ³⁄₄-inch strips
- 8 shelled raw shrimp
- 4 scallions, sliced in ½-inch sticks
- a small handful of cilantro leaves

1 Put the noodles in a pan or heatproof bowl, pour boiling water over them, and let soak for 1-2 minutes until softened. Drain and rinse under cold water, and set aside.

2 Heat a nonstick wok or frying pan until very hot, then spray with oil. Add the garlic and chiles and stir-fry for 30 seconds. Add the chicken and noodles and toss to combine. Stir-fry for 2 minutes.

3 Pour in the beaten egg and toss to combine.

4 Add the soy sauce, oyster sauce, sugarsnaps, and cabbage, and stir for 2 minutes.

5 Add the bean sprouts, squid, and shrimp, and cook for another 3-4 minutes, just until the shrimp are pink. Serve immediately, garnished with scallions and cilantro leaves.

PER SERVING: 325 calories; 4g fat; 0.7g saturated fat; 47g carbohydrate; 0.46g sodium

venison cutlets
on spring greens with blackberry sauce

Here the venison steaks are beaten thin to tenderize them – it also means that they will cook faster. The easiest way to pound the meat is to put it between two pieces of plastic wrap then, using a rolling pin or wooden mallet, beat it firmly, working from the centre of the meat outwards to flatten it.

SERVES 4

- **2 cups blackberries**
- **3 tablespoons cider vinegar**
- **1¼ cups fresh beef stock**
- **1 tablespoon olive or canola oil**
- **4 scallions, chopped**
- **18 ounces spring greens, finely shredded**
- **3 tablespoons slivered almonds, toasted**
- **4 x 4-ounce venison steaks (either from loin or haunch), beaten thin**
- **freshly ground black pepper**
- **1 tablespoon red currant jelly**
- **chopped chives, for garnishing (optional)**
- **14 ounces new potatoes, cooked and drained, for serving**

1 In a blender, puree half the blackberries with the cider vinegar and all but ¼ cup of the stock until smooth, then strain it through a fine mesh strainer to remove the seeds.

2 Pour the blackberry puree into a saucepan and cook over a medium heat until reduced to 1 cup – about 15 minutes. Set aside.

3 Heat half the oil in a large pot, add the scallions and cook for 1 minute. Add the reserved ¼ cup stock and the spring greens and stir to combine. Cover and cook over a medium heat for 7 minutes until the greens have wilted. Fold in the toasted almonds.

4 Meanwhile, heat the remaining oil in a large nonstick frying pan. Season the venison generously with pepper and cook the cutlets over a high heat for 1½ minutes each side. Cook them in two batches if necessary. Set aside but keep warm.

5 Add the red currant jelly to the venison pan with a couple of spoonfuls of blackberry sauce, scraping up any bits stuck to the bottom of the pan. Add the remaining blackberry sauce with the reserved blackberries and cook until the jelly has melted. Check the seasoning.

6 Spoon the greens onto four warm plates and surround with the blackberries and their sauce. Top the greens with the venison and sprinkle with chives, if you like. Serve with warm new potatoes.

PER SERVING: 400 calories; 13g fat; 1g saturated fat; 35g carbohydrate; 0.27g sodium

sunday pot roast

This reduced-calorie pot roast is sure to become a favorite in your household.

SERVES 6

- 2¼-pound piece boneless and skinless pork loin, excess fat removed
- 2 teaspoons dried sage
- freshly ground black pepper, to taste
- 2 large onions, each cut in 6 pieces
- 18 ounces sweet potatoes, cut in chunks
- 18 ounces carrots, scrubbed, cut in chunks
- 1¼ cups unsweetened apple juice
- 2 dessert apples, cored and each cut into 6 wedges
- 14 ounces fine green beans, cooked

1 Preheat the oven to 375ºF. Wipe the meat, then sprinkle the surface of the fat with half the sage and season with pepper. Set it in an ovenproof casserole dish, cover, and cook for 30 minutes.
2 Add the onions, sweet potatoes, carrots, apple juice, and the rest of the sage, and return to the oven for 45 minutes until the vegetables are almost tender.
3 Add the apple wedges and return to the oven for 15 minutes more. Test the meat with a skewer to make sure that it is cooked, then remove from the oven and let it rest for about 15 minutes before carving.
4 Serve with the green beans.

PER SERVING: 339 calories; 7g fat; 2g saturated fat; 41g carbohydrate; 0.11g sodium

baked turkey and vegetable pilaf

SERVES 4

- spray oil
- 1 onion and 1 garlic clove, both finely chopped
- 1 teaspoon soft thyme leaves
- 2 bay leaves
- 1 teaspoon ground coriander
- 1 teaspoon ground cumin
- 1 teaspoon turmeric
- ½ teaspoon chili powder
- 9 ounces turkey fillet, cut in strips
- 2 leeks, sliced
- 2 large carrots, sliced
- 9 ounces butternut squash, cut into chunks
- scant cup brown basmati rice, rinsed
- 2 cups chicken stock
- ¾ cup frozen peas
- 3 tomatoes, finely chopped
- 4 tablespoons chopped cilantro or parsley
- freshly ground black pepper, to taste

1 Preheat the oven to 350ºF. Set a heavy ovenproof pot over a medium heat and spray the inside with oil. Add the onion and garlic and cook gently for 5 minutes, adding a splash of water as necessary. Add the thyme, bay leaves, and spices. Stir then add the turkey and toss to coat with the spice mixture. Cook for 2 minutes.
2 Add the leeks, carrots, and butternut squash and cook for 3 minutes, then add the rice, stock, peas, and tomatoes. Bring to a boil, cover, and cook in the oven for 30-40 minutes until the rice is tender and most of the liquid has been absorbed.
3 Remove from the oven and fluff up the rice. Cover with the lid again and leave it for 3-5 minutes. Fold in the herbs, season with pepper, and serve.

PER SERVING: 350 calories; 5g fat; 0.7g saturated fat; 54g carbohydrate; 0.4g sodium

spicy vegetable curry

Many people think that curries are difficult to make, but that's not necessarily the case as most of them use only five main spices which you can keep in your cupboard at all times. Like most curries, this will freeze well—but don't freeze the rice.

SERVES 4

- 1 tablespoon canola oil
- 2 onions, each cut in 8 wedges through the root
- 4 garlic cloves, crushed
- 1 teaspoon ground cumin
- 2 teaspoons ground coriander
- 1 teaspoon turmeric
- $\frac{1}{2}$ teaspoon chili powder
- 1 teaspoon garam masala
- 1 teaspoon freshly ground black pepper
- $\frac{1}{2}$ cup green or brown lentils, rinsed
- 1 medium sweet potato, cut in 1-inch chunks
- 1 medium eggplant, cut in $\frac{1}{2}$-inch chunks
- 1 cup button mushrooms, wiped
- 3 tomatoes, cut in wedges
- 1 large handful baby spinach leaves
- $\frac{2}{3}$ cup no-fat yogurt
- 1 tablespoon cilantro leaves
- $1\frac{3}{4}$ cups cooked brown basmati rice

1 Heat the oil in a large pot, add the onions and garlic, and cook over a medium heat for 8-10 minutes until softened and without too much color.

2 Add the spices and cook until they smell aromatic – about 2 minutes. Add the lentils and stir to combine, then add the sweet potato and eggplant and cook for 5 minutes. Pour in $2\frac{1}{2}$ cups water, bring to a simmer, then cook, covered, for another 15 minutes.

3 Add the mushrooms and cook for 8 minutes, then stir in the tomatoes and spinach. Cook for 5 minutes, adding extra water as necessary to give a thick sauce consistency.

4 Fold in the yogurt and cilantro. Serve with the freshly cooked rice.

PER SERVING: 410 calories; 6g fat; 1g saturated fat; 76g carbohydrate; 0.18g sodium

Asian calf's liver with vegetables

Asian flavors work so well with liver. This recipe is particularly good with calf's liver, but lamb's liver or chicken liver are good substitutes.

SERVES 4

- **14 ounces calf's liver cut in ³/₄-inch strips**
- **4 scallions, very finely chopped**
- **1 garlic clove, crushed**
- **¼ teaspoon dried red pepper flakes**
- **1 teaspoon sesame oil**
- **2 tablespoons reduced-salt soy sauce**
- **2 teaspoons honey**
- **1 tablespoon cornstarch**
- **1 tablespoon canola oil**
- **2 carrots, thinly sliced**
- **9 ounces button mushrooms, quartered**
- **7 ounces sugarsnap peas, trimmed**
- **3cm piece of fresh ginger, peeled and finely shredded**
- **1 cup cooked brown basmati rice**
- **cilantro leaves, for garnishing**

1 Put the liver in a large bowl, then add a quarter of the scallions, the garlic, red pepper flakes, sesame oil, soy sauce, honey, and cornstarch, and toss to combine. Cover and leave to marinate for at least 1 hour or up to 24 hours in the fridge.

2 Heat a nonstick wok, then add half the oil and stir-fry the carrots for 1 minute. Add the mushrooms and sugarsnap peas and cook for another 1 minute over a high heat. Pour in ¼ cup water, cover the wok, and cook for 1 minute more. Transfer to a bowl and set aside.

3 Wipe out the wok with paper towels, then place over a high heat and add the remaining oil. Add the ginger and remaining scallions. Stir-fry for about 30 seconds, stirring continuously, then add the liver and its marinade and cook for 1 minute, stirring all the time.

4 Add a splash of water to the liver to moisten it, then return the vegetables to the wok and stir-fry for 1-2 minutes until all the ingredients are very hot.

5 Serve at once in warm bowls with the rice, garnished with cilantro leaves.

PER SERVING: 308 calories; 11g fat; 2g saturated fat; 31g carbohydrate; 0.45g sodium

FOR WEIGHT MAINTENANCE

Asian meatballs
with raw tomato sauce

A pleasant alternative to the classic Italian meatball dish, fresher, lighter, and containing all those Asian flavors. You can freeze the meatballs if you want.

SERVES 4

- 18 ounces lean ground pork
- 1 scallion, finely chopped
- 1 garlic clove, finely chopped
- 1¼-inch piece of fresh ginger, peeled and grated
- finely grated zest of 1 lime
- 2 tablespoons chopped cilantro
- 1 tablespoon fish sauce (nam pla)
- 1 small dessert apple, cored, grated, and excess juice squeezed out
- 1 tablespoon sweet chili sauce
- 1 tablespoon chopped cashews
- 9 ounces rice or buckwheat noodles or quinoa spaghetti (pictured)
- shredded scallions, for garnishing

FOR THE RAW TOMATO SAUCE

- 3 plum tomatoes, finely chopped
- 1 red chile, seeded and finely chopped
- 1 small red onion, finely chopped
- juice of 1 lime
- 3 tablespoons chopped cilantro
- 1 tablespoon canola oil

1 Preheat the oven to 400°F. For the meatballs, combine all the ingredients except the noodles and scallion in a mixing bowl. With wet hands, shape the mixture into small balls. Place in a roasting pan lined with baking parchment and cook in the oven for about 15 minutes, turning over once or twice, until opaque and cooked through.

2 Meanwhile, cook the noodles or pasta according to the package instructions. Combine all the ingredients for the raw tomato sauce. Mix the two together and let the pasta warm the sauce.

3 Divide the pasta between four warm bowls and top with the meatballs and shredded scallions.

PER SERVING: 449 calories; 11g fat; 3g saturated fat; 57g carbohydrate; 0.48g sodium

desserts

Yes, you can have your cake and eat it. These desserts are only about 100 calories or less, and will finish off any meal. They are based on fruit, so you will also be getting one of your five-a-day quota – another great reason to try these recipes. Choose the berry desserts in summer and the pumpkin recipe later in the year, while the bacoffee pots are sophisticated enough for any dinner party.

souffléed pumpkin pie custards

This recipe takes its inspiration from the great American tradition of making pumpkin pie. Not only does it taste good, but it is another way to get some vegetables into your daily diet.

MAKES 6

- 1 x 15-ounce can solid pack pumpkin
- finely grated zest and juice of 1 orange
- 1 teaspoon ground cinnamon
- ½ teaspoon ground ginger
- pinch of ground cloves
- 2 tablespoons maple syrup
- ⅔ cup lowfat milk
- 1 egg, separated
- 1 teaspoon confectioners' sugar, for dusting

1 Preheat the oven to 350ºF.
2 Beat together all the ingredients except the egg white until smooth. Whisk the egg white until stiff then fold through the mixture. Divide between six 6-ounce custard cups.
3 Set the custard cups in a roasting pan and pour enough boiling water into the pan to come at least halfway up the sides of the custard cups.
4 Bake for 20-25 minutes, until lightly set and warmed through. Serve warm, sprinkled with confectioners' sugar.

PER SERVING: 77 calories; 2g fat; 0.6g saturated fat; 12g carbohydrate; 0.08g sodium

summer berry fruit jello

Top these with a small scoop of plain yogurt or fromage frais and a bunch of red currants or a tiny sprig of mint, lemon balm, or sweet cicely.

SERVES 4

- about 4 sheets gelatin (or enough to set 2½ cups)
- 1¾ cups light cranberry juice
- ⅓ cup diet ginger ale
- 2 cups assorted berries: choose from small strawberries, raspberries, blackberries, blueberries
- 4 tablespoons fromage frais or plain yogurt (optional)
- 4 sprigs of mint or lemon balm (optional)

1 Soak the gelatin sheets in cold water according to the instructions on the package.
2 Warm half the cranberry juice in a small saucepan. Squeeze the excess water from the gelatin and stir into the warmed liquid until dissolved. Stir in the remaining juice and the ginger ale.
3 Halve or quarter the strawberries as necessary then arrange half the berries in four small glasses and pour over half the jelly. Chill until set then add the remaining berries and pour over the remaining liquid jelly. (Note: If you put all the fruit and jelly in at once the fruit will float to the top rather than be interspersed through the jelly.)
4 Chill until set. To serve, decorate with the fromage frais and herbs, if wished.

PER SERVING: 78 calories; 1g fat; 0.7g saturated fat; 11g carbohydrate; 0.04g sodium

papaya and lime sherbet

The nicest texture is achieved with an ice cream maker. If you haven't got one, freeze the mixture in a rigid plastic container, then let it soften slightly and beat with an electric beater or pulse in a food processor until smooth. Freeze until required.

SERVES 4

- **2 papayas**
- **juice of 1 lime**
- **1/3 cup diet tonic water**
- **1/2 teaspoon Angostura bitters (optional)**

1 Cut the papayas in half and remove the seeds. Peel the fruit, roughly chop the flesh and place in a blender or food processor along with the lime juice. Puree until smooth.
2 Stir in the tonic water and bitters, if using, and transfer to an ice cream maker. Churn until frozen. Serve at once or freeze until required.

PER SERVING: 49 calories; 0.2g fat; 0g saturated fat; 12g carbohydrate; 0.01g sodium

Anna's iced berry crush

Almost like an instant cheesecake ice. Keep one of the store-bought packs of fruit in your freezer and you can have this simple yet delicious dessert ready in 5 minutes!

SERVES 4

- **1 cup frozen summer berry selection**
- **1 cup quark (a fresh, white cheese, slightly chalky in texture)**
- **2 tablespoons maple syrup**

1 Roughly crush the frozen berries in a food processor, or in a bowl.
2 Stir together the quark and maple syrup and fold the berries through just so they give a ripple effect. Serve at once.

PER SERVING: 80 calories; 0.1g fat; 0g saturated fat;

 **FOR WEIGHT MAINTENANCE**

Afghan cardamom puddings

A delicate and refreshing dessert for hot weather. Agar is a setting agent that does not require cold to set it – however these desserts should be kept covered in the fridge until you need them. Agar is suitable for vegetarians.

SERVES 4

- **2 cups lowfat milk**
- **8 green cardamom pods, bruised**
- **1 tablespoon sugar**
- **1 tablespoon agar flakes**
- **2/3 cup small green grapes, for decorating**

1 Pour the milk into a small saucepan and add the cardamom pods. Heat gently just until bubbles form on the surface of the milk where it touches the pan. Cover and let sit for 1 hour until cooled.
2 Stir in the sugar, then sprinkle the surface of the milk with the agar flakes. Warm gently without stirring, then, once warm, stir and simmer very gently for 3-5 minutes until the agar dissolves.
3 Strain to remove the cardamom, then divide between four small glasses. Leave it until set, then cover and chill until required.
4 Halve or quarter the grapes and spoon them on top of the puddings.

PER SERVING: 83 calories; 2g fat; 1g saturated fat; 12g carbohydrate; 0.06g sodium

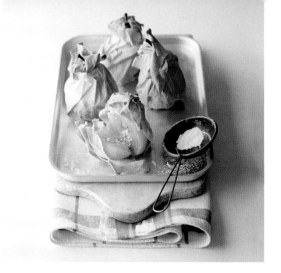

pears in nightshirts

Yes, you can eat pastry! The pears will soften and sweeten in the oven and will provide a contrasting texture to the crisp pastry.

SERVES 4

- **4 medium-ripe pears with stalks**
- **2 small balls preserved ginger, chopped**
- **2 tablespoons quark (see page 133)**
- **4 sheets (9½ x 19½ inches) phyllo pastry dough**
- **½ teaspoon confectioners' sugar**

1 Preheat the oven to 400ºF.

2 Peel and core the pears from the bottom, ensuring the stalks remain intact.

3 Mix together the ginger and quark and use to stuff each pear.

4 Brush one sheet of phyllo with a little water, then use it to encase a pear. Set on a nonstick baking tray. Repeat with the remaining phyllo and 3 pears.

5 Bake for 35-40 minutes until crisp and golden. You may need to turn them during cooking so that they bake evenly.

6 Put the confectioners' sugar in a sifter and sprinkle over the top of the pears. Serve at once.

PER SERVING: 111 calories; 1g fat; 0.1g saturated fat; 25g carbohydrate; 0.14g sodium

seared pineapple
with pomegranate salsa

Searing slices of pineapple on a ridged grill pan allows the natural sugars on the surface to caramelize – delicious.

SERVES 4

- **1 medium-sized pineapple**
- **¼ cup pomegranate seeds (or red currants or strawberries, chopped)**
- **1 tablespoon honey**
- **2 teaspoons chopped mint**
- **½ long red chile, seeded (optional)**

1 "Top and tail" the pineapple, then, using a sharp, serrated knife, cut away all the skin, removing the "eyes" – the black indentations – as you go.

2 Cut the pineapple into 10 even slices. Reserve the 8 best slices for grilling. Discard the core from the remaining 2 slices and chop the flesh finely. Mix with the pomegranate seeds, honey, and mint, and set aside.

3 Set a nonstick ridged grill pan or nonstick frying pan over a high heat. Sear the chile half just to soften it slightly, then finely chop. Add 1 teaspoon to the salsa (more if you prefer).

4 Sear the reserved slices of pineapple for about 1 minute each side until lightly golden. You will need to do this in batches.

5 Serve at once with the salsa.

PER SERVING: 76 calories; 0.3g fat; 0g saturated fat; 19g carbohydrate; 0g sodium

strawberry tart

Cook the pastry up to 4 hours before required, but add the topping just before serving.

SERVES 6

- **4 sheets phyllo pastry dough**
- **2 teaspoons unsalted butter, melted**
- **1 tablespoon confectioners' sugar**
- **6 tablespoons fat-free fromage frais or lowfat yogurt**
- **1 tablespoon lemon curd**
- **12 ounces small strawberries, hulled and cut in half**

1 Preheat the oven to 400ºF. Set a sheet of phyllo on a nonstick baking tray. Brush with a little melted butter and sprinkle with a little confectioners' sugar. Repeat the layers three more times, reserving about 1 teaspoon of the sugar.
2 Bake the pastry for 10 minutes until golden. Let it go cold.
3 Mix the fromage frais with the lemon curd and spread over the pastry. Top with the strawberries and sprinkle with the reserved confectioners' sugar. Serve at once.

PER SERVING: 89 calories; 2g fat; 1g saturated fat; 16g carbohydrate; 0.13g sodium

fresh figs
with rosewater
foam gratin

Foam is very popular with chefs at the moment –this is my version to try at home. Rosewater is available in the baking section of supermarkets and in Indian grocery stores. Try using 2½ cups strawberries and 1 cup blueberries instead of the figs and raspberries as a variation.

SERVES 4

- **2 medium eggs**
- **2 tablespoons sugar**
- **2 tablespoons rosewater**
- **4 fresh figs**
- **1 cup fresh raspberries**

1 Half fill the bottom of a double boiler, cover with water, and bring to a simmer.
2 Put the eggs and sugar in the top of the double boiler and set it over the simmering water. Using a hand-held electric whisk, beat the eggs and sugar to a thick foam that holds the trail of the beaters. Beat in the rosewater a little at a time. Switch off the heat under the double boiler.
3 Preheat the broiler to high. Cut the figs into six wedges each and arrange in four individual gratin dishes or saucers, along with the raspberries. Spoon the rosewater foam over them.
4 Set them under the broiler for about 1 minute until lightly golden. Serve at once.

PER SERVING: 98 calories; 3g fat; 0.8g saturated fat; 14g carbohydrate; 0.04g sodium

PER SERVING (WITH STRAWBERRIES AND BLUEBERRIES): 95 calories; 3g fat; 0.8g saturated fat; 14g carbohydrate; 0.04g sodium

apple galette

A galette is a French crêpe or flatcake that can be made with puff pastry dough, pancake batter, or a bread-like dough. I've used phyllo pastry dough here and a classic French topping.

SERVES 2

- 2 teaspoons raisins
- 2 sheets phyllo pastry dough
- 1 teaspoon unsalted butter, melted
- 1 dessert apple, cored, quartered, and very thinly sliced, then tossed with 1 teaspoon lemon juice
- 1 teaspoon pine nuts, toasted
- ½ teaspoon finely chopped fresh rosemary
- ½ teaspoon confectioners' sugar

1 Preheat the oven to 425ºF. Put the raisins in a small bowl, cover with boiling water, and set aside.
2 Brush each sheet of phyllo dough with water and fold in half. Set one on a nonstick baking tray, brush with water, and top with the second one. Bake for 10 minutes until lightly golden.
3 Brush the surface with melted butter. Casually arrange the apple slices to cover the surface of the pastry, then sprinkle with the pine nuts and rosemary. Sift the confectioners' sugar over the apples.
4 Bake the galette for 10 minutes until the apple is softened and the edges of the pastry are crispy and golden. Drain the raisins and sprinkle them over it. Serve at once.

PER SERVING: 118 calories; 4g fat; 2g saturated fat; 20g carbohydrate; 0.14g sodium

roasted peaches with blueberries

SERVES 4

- 3-4 (about 18 ounces) peaches
- 1 vanilla bean, split lengthwise
- large pinch of saffron strands
- ²/₃ cup white grape juice
- ²/₃ cup blueberries
- ¼ cup barley flakes
- 1 tablespoon sugar

1 Preheat the oven to 375˚F.
2 Quarter and pit the peaches and set them in a single layer in a baking dish. Add the vanilla bean, saffron, and grape juice, and bake, uncovered, for 20-30 minutes until tender. Switch off the oven.
3 Add the blueberries to the peaches and return to the oven to keep warm in the residual heat.
4 Meanwhile, toast the barley flakes in a nonstick frying pan over medium heat until lightly golden. Sprinkle in the sugar and let it melt. Stir well and let everything cold. Sprinkle the sugared flakes over the peaches and serve at once.

PER SERVING: 99 calories; 0.3g fat; 0g saturated fat; 24g carbohydrate; 0.01g sodium

stovetop plums

A quick and easy dessert.

SERVES 4

- 1 tablespoon unsalted butter
- 1 tablespoon light brown sugar
- 8 large red plums

1 Put the butter and sugar in a large nonstick frying pan over medium heat until melted.
2 Pit the plums, cut them in half, and add to the pan. Cover and simmer for 10-15 minutes until tender.

PER SERVING: 100 calories; 3g fat; 2g saturated fat; 18g carbohydrate; 0g sodium

FOR WEIGHT MAINTENANCE

basmati rice pudding
with apricots

A light rice pudding – basmati rice has a lower GI than normal pudding rice.

SERVES 4

- ¼ cup brown basmati rice
- ¼ cup lowfat milk
- 1 tablespoon light brown sugar
- 4 apricots, cut in half and pitted
- 1 fruit-flavored tea bag of your choice

1 Rinse the rice in a strainer under cold running water, then transfer to a saucepan and cover with 1¼ cups cold water. Let it soak for 30 minutes.

2 Bring to a simmer, then cover and simmer for 10-15 minutes until the rice is almost tender.

3 Add the milk and sugar and bring to a simmer. Simmer, covered, for 20-30 minutes, stirring occasionally until the rice is tender and the pudding has the consistency you like.

4 Meanwhile, put the apricot halves in a saucepan along with the tea bag and ⅔ cup cold water. Bring to a simmer, then simmer, covered, for 5-10 minutes until tender. Remove from the heat and discard the tea bag.

5 Serve the apricots with the rice pudding.

PER SERVING: 103 calories; 2g fat; 0.8g saturated fat; 20g carbohydrate; 0.06g sodium

FOR WEIGHT MAINTENANCE

mango fool (left)

Another very simple dessert recipe – it will make the perfect ending to a rich meal.

SERVES 4

- 1 large mango
- 200g lowfat fromage frais

1 Cut the two 'cheeks' from the mango and set aside.

2 Cut all the rest of the flesh from around the stone, discarding any skin. Purée in a liquidiser goblet, adding a little of the fromage frais, if necessary, then stir in the rest of the fromage frais.

3 Peel and dice the reserved mango 'cheeks' and layer up in four glasses with the puréed mixture. Serve at once or cover and chill until required.

PER SERVING: 100 kcals; 4g fat; 2g saturated fat; 13g carbohydrate; 0.02g sodium

FOR WEIGHT MAINTENANCE

bacoffee pots (right)

Little pots but lots of flavor!

SERVES 4

- 2 teaspoons instant espresso coffee
- 1 tablespoon dark brown sugar
- 1 large banana, mashed
- 1¼ cups fat-free fromage frais
- 2 tablespoons grated dark chocolate (72% cocoa solids)
- 2 teaspoons slivered almonds, toasted

1 Mix the coffee and sugar with 1 tablespoon boiling water to dissolve. Let it cool, then stir in the mashed banana and then fold in the fromage frais, keeping a slight ripple effect.

2 Transfer to four small glasses and chill until required. Top with chocolate and almonds before serving.

PER SERVING: 100 calories; 2g fat; 0.7g saturated fat; 16g carbohydrate; 0.02g sodium

Index

Index

CONVERSION CHART

WEIGHT (solids)		VOLUME (liquids)	
7g	¼ oz.	5ml	1 teaspoon
10g	⅓ oz.	15ml	1 tblsp or ½fl. oz.
15g	½ oz.	30ml	1fl. oz.
30g	1 oz.	45ml	1½fl. oz.
40g	1½ oz.	60ml	2fl. oz.
55g	2 oz.	90ml	3fl. oz. (⅓ cup)
70g	2½ oz.	100ml	3½fl. oz.
85g	3 oz.	120ml	4fl. oz. (½ cup)
100g	3½ oz.	150ml	5fl. oz.
115g	4 oz. (¼lb)	180ml	6fl. oz. (¾ cup)
125g	4½ oz.	240ml	8fl. oz. (1 cup)
140g	5 oz.	270ml	9fl. oz.
155g	5½ oz.	300ml	10fl. oz. (1¼ cups)
170g	6 oz.	330ml	11fl. oz.
200g	7 oz.	360ml	12fl. oz. (1½ cups)
225g	8 oz. (½lb)	410ml	14fl. oz. (1¾ cups)
255g	9 oz.	440ml	15fl. oz.
285g	10 oz.	480ml	16fl. oz. (2 cups)
300g	10½ oz.	500ml (0.5 liter)	17fl. oz.
310g	11 oz.	540ml	18fl. oz. (2¼ cups)
325g	11½ oz.	560ml	19fl. oz.
340g	12 oz. (¾lb)	600ml	20fl. oz. (2½ cups)
370g	13 oz.	650ml	22fl. oz. (2¾ cups)
400g	14 oz.	700ml	24fl. oz. (3 cups)
425g	15 oz.	820ml	28fl. oz. (3½ cups)
450g	16 oz. (1lb)	880ml	30fl. oz.
500g (½kg)	18 oz.	950ml	32fl. oz. (4 cups)
680g	24 oz. (1½lb)	1 liter	33.8fl. oz.
900g	32 oz. (2lb)	1.2 liters	5 cups
1kg	2¼lb	1.5 liters	50 fl. oz
1.1kg	2½lb	1.8 liters	7½ cups
1.2kg	2¾lb	2 liters	8½ cups
1.4kg	3lb		
1.5kg	3¼lb	**LENGTH**	
1.6kg	3½lb	5mm	¼ inch
1.8kg	4lb	1cm	½ inch
1.9kg	4¼lb	2cm	¾ inch
2kg	4½lb	2.5cm	1 inch
2.2kg	4¾lb	3cm	1¼ inches
2.3kg	5lb	4cm	1½ inches
		5cm	2 inches
		7.5cm	3 inches
		10cm	4 inches
		15cm	6 inches
		18cm	7 inches
		20cm	8 inches
		25cm	10 inches
		28cm	11 inches
		30cm	12 inches